WOODY SEZ

WOODY SEZ

By WOODY GUTHRIE

Preface by Studs Terkel

Compiled and edited by Marjorie Guthrie,
Harold Leventhal, Terry Sullivan,
Sheldon Patinkin.
With a Biography by Guy Logsdon

Publishers Grosset & Dunlap New York

The Woody Guthrie Tribute Fund has been established to perpetuate the memory of Woody Guthrie and to foster medical research into the causes and cures of Huntington's Disease and to sponsor a Woody Guthrie scholarship in folklore and folk music. For information on Woody Guthrie and the Woody Guthrie Tribute Fund, write to Room 2017, 250 West 57th Street, New York, N.Y. 10019.

Library of Congress catalog card number: 74-5623

ISBN 0-448-11759-2

First printing

Printed in the United States of America

Contents

Woody

Woodrow Wilson Guthrie was a tough little piece of leather — and an even tougher, bigger piece of man. It's no accident he became, in the words of Alan Lomax, "the greatest ballad-maker America has ever known." Hell, he was born July 14. That's Bastille Day, the celebration of something new — not yet arrived. The year was 1912. That's when the *Titanic* went down. An early sign that technology, arrogantly and presumptuously used, could not defy the ice of nature. Woody, of course, realized all this way back. That's why he sang of God giving Noah the rainbow sign that it wouldn't be water but fire next time. Being a poet, he was by his very nature a prophet.

The funny thing is he never regarded himself as unique. He believed everybody was unique. "You may have been taught to call me by the name of a poet, but I'm no more of a poet than you are. I am no more a writer of songs than you are, no better singer. The only story I've tried to write down has been you." He'd usually sign off in this manner: "Let me be known as just the man that told you something you already knew." Maybe so. But the way he told it and sang it and shouted it is what made him the nonpareil.

I remember a night in 1941. He and three colleagues, Pete Seeger among them, were passing through Chicago. They were on tour, singing everywhere and anywhere, wherever people were in trouble and trying to do something about it. Woody slipped off around 10 P.M. to a neighborhood tavern. About two in the morning — or was it three? — as though in a dream, I heard a rapid-fire tapping away on my portable. A few hours later, on awakening, I noticed the wastebasket rammed with foolscap, typed single-space. God, it was Joyceian, Burnsian, Wolfeian, O'Caseyian. Never had a neighborhood tavern been so overflowing with life and its wild comedy and its high hope. And so off-handedly chronicled. I have no idea what happened to that wastebasket, damn it.

Small matter. There was always more where that came from. Writing ballads came as natural to Woody as breathing. Anything man did or had done to him was the source. "Any event which takes away the lives of human beings, I try to write a song about what caused it to happen and how we can all try to keep such a thing from happening again." Or which takes away their sense of personal worth. That's what made Woody the most mad.

He hated to see people being constantly put down. By, say, a mechanical mouth, such as Bob Hope today. If there is a single thread running through all his works, it is precisely this. I paraphrase badly what he said on more than one occasion: I hate songs, I hate comments that make people feel they're no good because they're too fat or too skinny or because they're raggedy-dressed or because they're different. . . . So it was his songs bespoke not only hard truths but possibilities of some better way to look at one another. "Everybody talks at everybody and nobody listens to what anybody is saying." Make no mistake: his weren't sugar-candy songs. Nor were they cant. He saw what he saw and heard what he heard. And he put it all down, "to speak out what's rambling around in my own mind."

Aside from Steinbeck's *Grapes of Wrath* and Dorothea Lange's and Walker Evans' photographs, there is no better chronicle of hard times than Woody's Dust Bowl ballads. Nor are there more eloquent anthems to man's potential than his Columbia Valley songs. And always there was a sense of wonder and astonishment. That's why his songs for children are like no others written. As with all good poets, there was a child inside him, seeing all things afresh. That's why they are for now as well as then. At a time of such stunning banality as we now experience, his songs and writings are more than stirring. They are necessary. So is this book.

Studs Terkel

Poet of the people

Woody Guthrie was a man of many talents. He was a folk poet, folk singer, and author; he was a country boy in a big city, a family man who wandered, and an individualist with a worldly vision. He was one of the most influential, and yet generally unrecognized, creative spirits of the past thirty years, particularly in the urban folk revival. His life-style and personality evoked admiration and criticism, love and hatred.

Born Woodrow Wilson Guthrie on July 14, 1912, in Okemah, Oklahoma, to Charley and Nora Guthrie, Woody was the third of five children. As a child, he enjoyed the comforts and pleasures normally provided a family by a successful businessman of that time. His father was a politician as well as a farmer-stockman and real estate investor. His mother was both beautiful and talented. Her mother had been a frontier school teacher in Indian Territory and Nora was a singer of old songs. Charley and Nora were a good-looking couple with a promising future. But shortly after Woody was born tragedy struck.

Nora developed symptoms of Huntington's Disease, a congenital disease that attacks the central nervous system and debilitates the victim and for which there was and is no known cure. It progresses slowly and can result in an early death for its victim. The symptoms often are involuntary movements and depression that were formerly diagnosed as insanity. Nora was thought to be going insane and the family stability slowly disintegrated.

When Woody was six, his thirteen-year-old sister Clara died from burns; she was alone in the house when apparently kerosene on her clothing was ignited. This tragedy contributed to the dissolution of the Guthrie success and family. Fire also destroyed one of their homes, and later a tornado damaged another. Woody grew up in this progressing sadness, but he had a father who was a fighter and an optimist, two characteristics that were transmitted to Woody.

Woody's years in Okemah, a town of about two thousand at the time, had much influence on him. The town was developed overnight in 1902 as a railroad junction; it was a part of the Creek Indian Nation with much ranching interest and farming activity around it. Three all-black communities were founded in the county; and coal mining was a major industry twenty miles east of Okemah. When Woody was about ten, oil was discovered twelve miles southwest of the town, and since it was the nearest rail station, Okemah's population jumped to fifteen thousand almost overnight. However, within four years it was back to its original size with the scars of an oil boomtown. Combined with his community experience were the factors that his mother had come to Indian Territory from Kansas with Northern traditions and his father had come as a cowboy from south central Texas with Southern traditions. Also, Charley was a lifelong democrat. In short, Woody's life in Okemah was a cultural melting pot.

Following Clara's death, nothing seemed to go right for the family, and in June of 1927 Charley was seriously burned. Nora was committed to Central State Hospital, Oklahoma's mental hospital, where she died a few years later. Charley and the two youngest children moved to Pampa, Texas, to live with a sister while he recuperated. Woody and his older brother Roy stayed in Okemah.

For the next two years, Woody lived with various friends during the school year and traveled as a migrant agricultural laborer in the summers.

This experience was the beginning of a lifelong empathy with migratory laborers. In 1929, after his junior year in high school, he moved to Pampa to be with the family.

There he worked at a variety of occupations, learned to play the guitar from an uncle, played in a western swing band for dances and parties, married Mary Jennings and started a family, and experienced the fury of the dust storms that became known as the Dust Bowl era. Out of this Pampa experience came his Dust Bowl ballads.

In 1937, with a desire to become a western singer combined with his restless nature, Woody traveled to Los Angeles, where, over a variety of radio stations, he and some relatives and a friend,"Lefty Lou," sang. Their material was folk and country songs combined with a few original ones. His cousin Jack Guthrie was with him a short time, and in 1945 recorded a song that they had worked on together in Los Angeles, "Oklahoma Hills," which has become a country-western standard.

Woody's technique was to take old folk songs or tunes and write new words to them and to rework the melody when necessary. He was a poet, not a composer. Over one thousand songs were written by this technique, of which "This Land Is Your Land," "So Long, It's Been Good to

Know You," and "Philadelphia Lawyer" are the best known.

While in Los Angeles, Woody, like many artists during the Depression, became interested in the Communist Party. He wrote many articles for their publications, but he was too much of an uncontrollable and unpredictable individualist to fit completely into any particular party structure. But he worked hard for ideals and beliefs that he held.

In 1940, Woody, along with Will Geer, Lee Hays, and others in the growing folk movement, moved to New York City. That year Alan Lomax recorded a series of interviews with him for the Library of Congress most of which are now available from Elektra Records, and RCA released his "Dust Bowl Ballads" album. Also, he met Marjorie Mazia, who was a dancer with Martha Graham; she became his second wife and the mother of their four children, of whom Arlo has developed his own career in the music world. Their first child, Cathy, died of burns in 1947 at the age of four.

Woody's autobiographical novel *Bound for Glory* was published in 1943 by E. P. Dutton and Company. Clifton Fadiman wrote that Woody's talents were "a natural possession like Yellowstone and Yosemite," and that he was a new Walt

Whitman. During the war years, Woody served in the Merchant Marine, and three ships were torpedoed beneath him. He was drafted into the Army near the end of the War and served for nine months before being honorably discharged.

During these and the following years, he recorded for Folkways Records, which released numerous albums, and he worked and traveled with the Almanc Singers, Lee Hays, Burl Ives, Josh White, Leadbelly, Pete Seeger, Cisco Houston, Millard Lampell, and many other performers and artists. He wrote *American Folksong* in 1946. Just before his death some of his writings were edited and published as *Born to Win*.

In New York City Woody became more aware of his style and lost some of the unconscious style and spark that is a characteristic of folk art; he became more of a literary artist with an obsession to write. Woody was a great admirer of Will Rogers and had developed his style around the "illiterate" style of Rogers. In fact, his "Woody Sez" column was patterned after the "Will Rogers Says" column; and in it he deliberately used misspellings in an effort to recreate the speech patterns of the common people — those he knew best.

Woody's influence was a basic element in the folk revival of the 1950s led by Pete Seeger and the Weavers. He inspired Bob Dylan and influenced the folk-rock movement of the 1960s, and Woody continues to be heard in folk, rock, and country-western music. The Department of the Interior presented a Conservation Service Award to him in 1966 in recognition of his efforts "to make our people aware of their heritage and the land."

Woody's writing activities covered only a short span — fifteen years at most — for in the late 1940s he developed the symptoms of the disease that had killed his mother. In 1954 he was hospitalized, and only occasionally thereafter was he able to leave for short drives and visits. On October 3, 1967, after thirteen years of hospitalization, Woody died; but through his talents and concepts he will live as long as mankind sings, reads, and thinks. Equally important is the interest and attention that his life and death have focused on the necessity for research in Huntington's Disease and other genetic neurological disorders.

Woody's life was filled with tragedy, all uncontrollable and unpredictable, but at no time did he quit and give in to total despair. He continually expressed love for his native state, and for his country, and for all of mankind, and he was courageous enough to criticize what needed to be improved. His songs contained hope and humor to "make you feel good." Truly, this land is the land of a folk artist who was "born to win."

Guy Logsdon
University of Tulsa

Woody Sez

The articles collected here first appeared in a column in *People's World*, published in San Francisco, under the title "Woody Sez," from May 12, 1939 to January 3, 1940. *People's World* announced the column in this way:

Woodrow Guthrie or just plain Woody, as he is known to thousands of radio listeners, will be a daily feature in The People's World from now on.

Woody calls himself a hill-billy singer. He is one of the 200,000 people who came from the dustbowl looking for work and a little food — the people who have picked the fruit and the crops of California — lived in shanty camps, been beaten and driven about by the bank-landowners.

But Woody came with a guitar on his back and with an eye and an ear sensitive to the suffering of his own people.

He sings songs every day over KFVD from 2:15 to 2:45 and has many thousands of listeners and people who write him letters. He writes these songs himself.

And Woody has gathered a great deal of homely wisdom from his people. Every day he will speak to you on this page in his own way about how he looks at things.

woody guthrie

1 My people, the dustbowl refugees

Gawdamighty. I been interested in a world of stuff since I been born. Sold papers, shined shoes, polished spittoons, sold gas and oil, clerked in a hotel, picked that cotton, drilled waterwells, helped a carpenter, drilled wheat, drove tractors, bootlegged whiskey, peddled home brew, jerked soda, stocked groceries, painted signs, traveled in road shows, read hypnotism, studied human nature, tried to preach, played a guitar, sung in saloons, practiced divine healing, played in movies, rode freight trains, begged back doors, slept in a million jails, slept under bridges, broke my arm on a bronco, wrote junk, been from coast to coast the hard way, believe in everybody, joined everything, and still a goin strong. Above statements are all true.

Lots of ambitious young students wood like to knowe how u git a start at th' writin game . . . Which, of course, although, however, nevertheless, is as hungerey a game as you cood pick.

And, in the attitude that it is my duty to scatter enlightenment where, and when I can . . . I carve here what I wood say is the key secret of the art and science of a writing.

Just deecide what you want to write about. Then you deecide why you want to write about it.

Then you climb gently and sweetly up to your paper, and with pen, pencil, or typewriter thoroughly cocked and primed . . . just go ahead an' WRITE IT.

Awtowbiografie

Well, I was born in Okemah, Okfuskee County, Oklahoma, in 1912, the year that Woodrow Wilson was nominated for President. My dad was quite a figger in Okfuskee county politics at that time, and so he named me after the President, Woodrow Wilson Guthrie — which is too much of a name for a country boy. So I sawed off all the fancy work an' jest left "Woody" — I cood remember that.

Okemah got to be a oil boom town, just like about ½ the other towns down there, an' got to be full of boom-chasers, drillers, roustabouts, tool-dressers, teamskinners, bootleggers, Indian guardians, an' other tong-buckers an' grease monkeys of the oil field work. When Okemah went dead, I left town with the first migration, headed for the plains of west Texas, around Amarillo, Pampa, and Borger.

I worked several years in a drug store which turned into a likker store when prohibition went out. The boss of the likker store said that on that very day I took a greater liking to my work. Personal, I woodent say. Anyhow, in them oil boom towns, located as they was right in the big middle of the dust bowl, it was dern hard to find a place of business that wasn't engaged directly or indirectly in the bootleg game.

Migration

After all, the bootleg game had played a mighty important part in the history of Oklahoma. Lots of folks said that the main reason they voted whiskey back in, was so's they cood get Oklahoma's oil fields a way from the Indians.

If they's anything in any field of indeaver that I've accomplished, I don't know what it is.

When the drouths drove all the folks out of Oklahoma, an' Arkansaw, into the cow country, wheat fields, an' oil towns of West Texas, I was in the runoff. We had a hard old go of it. I've picked it by asking questions that the bad weather drove 1, an' the banker drove 9 out of every ten families thet deeserted there farms by the oodles an' gobs in eastern Okla., Arkl, Missouri, Kansas, Alabama, Georgia, Texas, an' Tennessee. (Naturally my stetistics is jest a guess, but a mighty good guess, I think.)

Matrimony

You know when the finance folks and the weather both set in on you at the same time, they ain't nothin' else to do but dessert the farm.

An, you know, when you cause a person to lose faith in old mammy earth, he has really lost a lot.

Well, I married a girl, as moste fellers did in them days. She was the blond-haired daughter of a family of Oklahoma farmers thet came from down around Hydro, an' Weatherford, Okla. We been married six or seven years (I don't know for shore) — but have got two little girls, Teeny, 3½, an Baby Sue, 1½.

Handy Man

We wrestled with the dust storms there in Texas till we wore the house out a tryin' to keep it clean, an' finally rented it out to a colony of ground hogs for a prairie dog hotel.

I worked as a grocery clerk, shelf-stocker, banner painter, windo and customer trimmer, an' all-around clean-up man.

I got what you wood call disgursted, busted, and rooled me up a bundel of duds, an' caught a long-tail, frate-train thet had a California sign on

the side of it. I got down in a refrigerater car, "reefer" — somewhere in the dustbowl — an' the first daylight I seen, it said California 121314151 feet below sea level.

Roving Man

I was a headin' out to see some relatives, but I diden't know for shore wich r.r. bridge they was a livin' under, so you see I was a travelin' practically without a magneto. I mean a compass. I diden't know where the heck I was a goin'.

So when the police asked me where I was a goin' — I jest asked 'em where a good California town was, an' hooked up, an' went to it. In this way you can rest easy every night cause you ain't goin' nowheres in the mornin' anyway.

I'd jest stand out by the highway, an' stick both thumbs up, an' whichever way I went, was maternal to me. I diden't give a hoot.

Radio Hit

Anyway, I seen about 99 44-100 of California's great senery, from Tia Juana to the Redwood forests, from Reno, an' Lake Tahoe, to the Frisco bay. I finally fooled around an' found my relatives up at Turlock, Calif., an et off of them till we all picked up an' moved down to Lost Angeles — where we've been ever since.

I was asked here a while back how come me to ever git started on the radeo, an' I says, I swan, I don't know. I jest went down to the feller's office, an' I says, how about it? An' he says okay, and so, with other difrent singers an' musicians, who done most of the good work, I've made this electrified racket for a bout fourteen months.

I was kindly asked and kindly agreed to do some writin' for the Olson newspaper, Light, because they thot I mite have a Hillbilly's Eye-View of the hole Migratious Labor movement from the South to the Pacific Coast. An' because I figgered it wood be helpful to my people, the dustbowl refugees, I was tickled to get the chanct.

"World" Bit

And, so, in a gettin' acquainted with you readers of The People's World, I ain't got much to say. The reason I ain't got much to say is because I've been a tryin' to rite about myself, an' when a feller is a tryin' to talk about his self, he'd might just as well say nothin.

Anyhow, if you will, an can, read what I rite —
I'm mighty glad to be a writin' it.

Dont be bashful a bout writing to me if you
know of a job. I play the guitar and am what is
known as a Magical Singer, in as much as I fool
the audience completely. I keep them guessing all
during the show — why the devil they bought a
ticket.

I am the one and only right handed left handed
entertainer in the field; and have been told I'd be
better in the field, with a hoe. I've dug with a
hoe, but I can raise more cain by digging the re-
publicans.

If you are afraid I woodent go over in your
lodge or party, you are possibly right. In such
case just mail me $15 and I wont come. When I
perform I cut it down to $10. When for a good
cause, $5. When for a better cause, I come free. If
you can think of a better one still, I'll give you my
service, my guitar, my hat and 65¢ cash money.

After an original drawing by Woody Guthrie

2 And the government is the people

Ed Robbin & Byron Dunham was ahaving somewhat of a gentlemenly argument about some high fangled terms — about the various planes or phases of consciousness one goes thru (in becoming plumb conscious) among others of which they talked of class consciousness.

Now Ed & Byron was plumb out of my territory a using them high falutin words, but I enjoyed the consciousness as much as they did.

I walked into the room where they was, an Byron he up and says, "Now you take Woody here, he aint a bit class conscious, are you Woody?"

An Ed says, "Why shore, he's class conscious — why you woodent know a class conscious feller if you met him in the road."

An then they asked me, "What do you think policemen is hired to do, pertect rich folks property, or safeguard the widows an orphens?"

An I says, well, what few policemen I ever knowed — was more or less hired — I reckon to pertect rich folks property — an then the widows an orphens, too.

I never stopped to think of it before, but you know — a policeman will jest stand there an let a banker rob a farmer, or a finance man rob a workin man.

But if a farmer robs a banker — you wood have

After an original drawing by Woody Guthrie

After an original drawing by Woody Guthrie

a hole dern army of cops out a shooting at him.

Robbery is a chapter in ettiquette.

CRIME IS ON THE INCREASE . . . so they tell me.

Personal, I dont know if it is 'er aint. I am inclined to think it aint. I dont know why.

Eny how, if it is, it wont be long till things will come to a funny fix.

The papers will not read: MAN GETS PRISON TERM.

They'll read: MAN FOUND IN PRISON.

If they keep on a passin' laws, a day wont blow by, but what you'll break some dern fool law, an' be liable fer a life time prison term about it. Learned authorities tell me now days that ever body in the U.S. breaks at least a dozen jail house offences every day . . . sommers in the U.S.

Well, as many laws as they got wrote up, I woodent doubt it, an' at the present rate they're passin laws, they'll soon have it against th' law to even pass a law . . . then all of us will be in the same jail.

All we got to do is build a great big wall around the world, an' put bars in it, an' then we're all in the hoosegow.

½ of the laws that's passed now days helps to

put the gangsters in jail. The other helps to get him out again. Goes to show what money can do. Money, you know, is power, I dare say — as powerful as prayer. Because, the old familiar smell of some greenback money will quickly alter, 'er change the prayer of a very prayerful man.

We hire fellers to make laws. We hire fellers to change laws. We hire fellers to break laws. We marry into a bunch of in-laws (which we refer to as outlaws), an' how the heck we stay out of the pen is more than I can see.

Course I only got a 1 cylinder brain . . . you work on it . . . (not too hard though).

WASHINGTON. — Boy look what I'm into. Some town Washington. That's where you go to make laws, break laws, rake laws, fake laws, take laws, and shake laws.

Seen the original copy of the Constitution, which was fine. I was interested to know if they still had it. It was fading out purty fast, the ink was a gettin dimmer and dimmer, so they waxed it and sprayed it and sanded it and polished it and put it in a case behind some yellow glass. I'm dam glad they preserved it before it faded plumb out. But you still got to get awful clost to it before you can get the real good out of it.

A SENATOR is something very few people know about. Not even the Senaters know 'em. An the Repersentatives knows less about em. When you see a man that dont know what he wants to do, and he dont know when he wants to do it, an never does do it after all — well, you can jest say. There's a Sanater. If he aint one, you cood suggest to him thet he git on the next ticket. In all probability, he'd be elected.

A Senator is a man — who has taken a trip to the Capital, to make the acquaintance of a group of men who've made the same trip. When some $$ money is set aside for Relief, a Senator sez, I aint seen it, have you senate? An' the other Senators say, Nope, we aint senate, have you senate?

The Housewives of the country are always afraid at nite, afraid they's a Robber in the House. Nope, Milady most of em is in the Senate.

I tuned in Sunday on the radeo an heard a hole tribe of senaters a making speeches — on ever conceivable subjict under the sun, an' though the manner in which they brought forth their arguments, their polished wit, and subtle maneuvers, were all very entertaining, I come out of it as empty handed as i went in.

a libral is a
feller that
wood like to
git his hands
on somethin to
give to the
poore . . . . .

After an original drawing by Woody Guthrie

It was sort of like a hearin' the hens a cacklin' — and a running out to th barn — an' findin all of th' old clucks in a funny state of straining — loud, noisy, and plenty entertaining — but no eggs.

I am, it is true, more aware of what they are arguin' a bout, but the reverse is all so true — that of the solution, i aint no wiser.

One Senator jumped up an told the National Debt in 1937. He made it look like we dident owe nobody nothin' — (and, in my heart of hearts, i a gree with him) — but about thet time, up jumped a nother senator, an' proved conclusively thet the figgers th' (gentleman from down th' river) had jest read — was not the figgers of 1937, but of more then 10 years ago.

So if them senaters caint come no closeter to agreement then that, an' gits as bawled up as them radeo speeches was, i rest in the silence of sweet assurance that youre guess, as my guess (farmers, workers, hoboes, hoodlums, preachers, screechers, gamers, framers, women-tamers, priests, angles, outlaws, slaves, monks, nuns, landlords, knaves . . .). Their guess, i mean. Youre guess . . . . is, by george, as good as eny!

I gawthered the Reactionary Replubicans was in love with the Reactionary Replubicans; also that the Liberal Demacrats was in love with th' Liberal Demacrats.

Each presented a brief case of statstics proving that the other brief cases of stastics, was mistaken, misread, misquoted, mislabeled, and mis-spoken.

One New Dealer whittled the National Debt down to a paltry $2345678904321, 450938356471823456 — an' then showed thet instead of me a owin' myself $798, I really had twelve cents a comin'.

The national debit is one thing I caint figger out. I heard a senator on a radeo a saying that we owed somebody 15 jillion dollers. I don't know their name, but I remember the price. Called it the national debit. If the nation is the government, and the government is the people, then I guess the people owes the people, that means I owe me, and you owe you, and I forget the regular fee, but if I owe myself something, I would be a willing just to call it off rather than have the senators argue about it, and I know you would do the same and then we wouldn't have no national debit.

One night a hobo friend of mine come up to where we was all a standing and he said he knew about a good warm place to sleep. He got quite a follering. In fact it was e pluribus Union. Well, he led us off down the r. r. tracks about a half a mile and we come to an old shack built out of roof lumber, with great big cracks and you could see through . . . about to fall over . . . looked like a republican platform. The reason I so strongly call it a republican platform is because ever body went there to sleep. The reason why I go so far as to compare it even more closely with a republican platform was because it looked like you could rest there, but you couldn't. They had hired guards and things and big harness bulls to whim wham the fool out of you. And wear their own selfs out doing it.

THEM: AFTER ALL
WHAT IS MONEY?
US: DERN IF I
KNOW — NEVER
HAD ANY !

After an original drawing by Woody Guthrie

3 Kids first.
Hoboes second.
Rich folks last

WELL, in the first place, you got to have a definition for "Relief" —

And here's a Definition for Relief:

Relief, (noun),: It is 2 people and one of them has accumulated the property of both; and then poses as some sort of a "giver" — when in reality he is only giving back a little at a time, the Life that he took at a single grab or two. . .

Most like a poker game where the cards is marked — and set and shuffled and "dealt", and timed, and framed, and organized and arranged to "relieve" you of what you got — and then turned around and gives you a mess of beans in exchange for your Freedom, — and then make a big speech or two about it and call it "Relief."

They first relieve you of what you got, then "Relief" you for what you get.

They tell me the rich folks is a gonna give us a little relief quick as they can find a way to do it without a lowerin the standard of a livin —

Shux most of us aint never seen no standard yet.

I seen it once over at a friends house.

But I coodent appreciate it fer thinkin of the folks that aint got it.

The standard of a living is a home, an a car, an a lectric ice box, an clothes, an radeo, an groceries, an wages you can live on, an some spair time to loaf, an some spair money to spend.

An some other stuff I forgot.

Anyway, you aint got it an neither have I.

But the folks that has got it got it from you an me. An when the highups can invent a way to give you four bits and get back a dollar you will get some relief.

I'm a standing here a looking at the trees and the rocks, and reckon what that reminds you of to write about? Well, trees is full of groceries, that's for something to eat. And the rocks is hard — that's how hard it is to get, and they's lots of trees and they's lots of rocks, and just between the two, I'd say folks is between a grub-stake and a hard place. It looks like some folks spend three fourths of their life a learning how to buy and wear and eat clothes and grub, and most of us got to beat our heads against the rocks to try to get a hold of either.

The Times carried quite a story about the flood, drouth, an' dust-bowlers a comin' to Calif. in their rickety, rundown jallopies, their little handful of belongin's, an' their children . . . only, says the Times, to dig into some of the Relief Gold.

The tale, written by Kenneth Somebody, an' paid for by Mr. Somebody Else, was wrote up for the one purpose of givin' the Refugees another black eye.

The Migratious Workers was compared to Hollywood, Reno, and Wilshire Gold-Diggers . . . only the "Gold" thet the Workers dug, was sposed to come from the Taxpayers' & Property Owners' stach.

The story was spun around the conditions of the Refugees a livin' in the various Trailer Cities thet are strung around over the country, the conditions in which the children must live in destitution, want, filth and despair.

Scenes or Life in a Trailer Camp City were painted to call your attention to the untold, inhuman suffering that these people are willing to go thru — just for some of that "Easy Relief Money."

How the Sheriff's Force "cleared out the Jungles," and drove the Shack dwellers out of the River Bottom, set fire to their Cardboard houses, and destroyed their patch-work shelters — was told about — not to make you feel in your heart a genuine sorrow for your brothers and sisters of our American Race that's got to live in such places, but to try to make you believe that these Underprivileged people are designing in their hearts to "Dig some Easy Gold" — off you Taxpayers.

The Author was trying to make you believe that these weatherbeaten, browbeaten, homeless people are really robbers at heart and he gave some typical conversations of some Oklahoma people who were living like wild hogs in a boggy river bottom for a whole year in order to get some of that easy Relief Gold.

No, Kenneth . . . it ain't the "Easy Relief Money Us Folks Is After" — it's jest a chanct to work an' earn our livin' . . . sorta like you earn youre livin'. You've got yore gift of Writin' — an' that's the way you work an' earn yore meal ticket here in this old world. An' each one of us has got our little Job thet we hope to do in order to pay for our keep.

We can gather in the crops. An' we can drive Tracters, an' Draglines, an' Shovels, an' Cranes, an' Cement Mixers, an' Picks, an' Hammers, an' lots of things like that.

'Course we ain't as educated as you are — 'cause you're a mighty smart feller. But we'd like fer our children to grow up an' be big, smart, educated fellers like you. ('Course if any of 'em ever got so educated thet they took to a robbin' or a runnin' the rest of the folks down, or a makin' fun of the pore folks — well, we jest naturally wooden't claim him no more.)

Personal, I've ben in Calif. 2 years — 'cause the dust and the cold, run me out of Texas . . . an' I ain't never applied for relief of any kind yet. An' for the past year I've averaged a makin' less than $1 a day.

But before I'd make my livin' by a writin' articles that make fun of the Hungery Folks, an' the Workin' Folks,

I'd go on Relief. . .

Yrs Trly Woody

I GOT A RELATIVE THAT THINKS YOU CAN BEAT TH HOSS RACES. Well, you meet all sorts an sizes of people.

I seen a big signe board a few days a go that said Races to day at Hollerwood Park — all proceeds to Chairyt — how do you spell Cah — Chairity???

Enyhow — I was just a wonderin why you coodent put in some government race hosses, an let all of th proceeds go to th poore folks — ever day — enstead of oncet a coons age. All you wood have to do wood be to breed a string of government hosses that was class concsious, an explane to each horse that ever time you win a race, you build a hosspital — an I think they'd turn out faster an better then th capital plugs we got a hoffin — hoofin — now days.

You know — the comin times will perduce hosses better an faster then th ones you got now — an itll be cause you put better idees in th hosses head. Yessir what we need is govt hoss races an let ever race go to put up a orphens home — or a county hosspital — or a swimmin pool, or somethin.

Everywhere a poor feller looks, they is a Finance Co starin you right in th face. An th big banks is a keepin em in busness so's they can give you four bits, an git back a dollar — an boost youre hours up an cut youre wages down, an give you a skinnin ever time you turn a round, an salute th flag, an call it freedom.

Lots of folks dont know all they is to know about Wall St.

Wall St. is the st. that runs to the kitchen on the pockit book of ever American home.

One stomack ache on Wall St. can empty the pockitbook an kitchen.

One case of roomatisem on Wall St. can close down 100 factories.

One bad cold on Wall St. can close down 1000 shops.

One sneeze on Wall St. can put a whole army of workers on the bum.

This is a pushbutton civilization an Wall St. is where the button is.

Wall St. is where the workers git worked on an the reapers git reaped — an the farmers git plowed under.

Wall St. is a st in N.Y. It's where the Robbers go to get Robbed. Just when you get to a thinkin' you're purty slick robber, an' a littel smarter then the others, why you take a notion to go up to Wall St., an boy — you come back, but your money don't.

Wall St. is the St. where the Big Refagees eats the Little Refagees up. Wall St. is the reason why you got Refagees. Wall St. is the St. which is the reason why a pore hard working man caint ever break even.

Wall St. is the St. which is why you owe everybody an' his dog. An' ever Finance & Salary Lone Outfit from Cape Cod to Hickory Bend is a blood vessel runnin' up to Wall St.

Wall St. is the St. where instead of Pickpockets, you got a bunch of blank-lookin' Specalaters a usin' the money you lent em to rob

WE PLEGE OUR ALEGIANCE TO OUR FLAG ...... AN TO WALL ST., FOR WHICH IT STANDS .....ONE DOLLAR, UNGETTABLE .....

After an original drawing by Woody Guthrie

you of the pocket change you kept for carfare. They lug enough gold bricks into and out of them Wall St. doors ever day to bring Prosperity back in 40 minutes, an' keep Progress a goin' fer a thousend; but they go ahead, a lugin the Prosperity in one door an th Progress out of a nother door, and it dont never get 50 ft. from where it is.

You mite say Wall St. is the St. thet keeps you off of Easy St.

What Wall Street is a lookin fer is a humen being to put out in front — to front for em — the reason for this is cause you caint hardly find none on Wall St. I mean no humens.

When youre mind gits to where it rangs like a cash register ever time you think, why you wood make a good hand on Wall St., but you woodent make a good enything else.

That reminds me of the one about the one eyed banker that spent a young fortune buying himself the best glass eye that could be made. It was finished and he went around betting everybody that you couldn't tell which was the glass eye and which was the real eye. He was dealing with a farmer, buying a load of tomatoes, and the banker bet him $100, and laid it down. The farmer looked at the banker for a minute, and pointed out the glass eye. The banker lost. The farmer won. "Tell me — how did you pick the glass eye?" The banker wanted to know. And the farmer remarked, "Well 'y gad, ye see, I jest went to a lookin' fer th' eye that had a little gleam of life an' friendliness fer us farmers in it — an' I knowed dern well that it would be — th' Glass One . . . "

The only success I ever had in comfort was to try to make comfortable the place I was. I dident all ways succeed but the comfort comes from a trying — not from the comfort. Comfort aint so much to be found in comfort as it is in the work you go through to find it.

Most everything in the world is made for comfort — homes, ice boxes, stoves, furniture, chairs, beds, covers, radeos an phonografs, clothes, shoes, hats, cosmetics, lipstick, hats (hats again), tobaccer, ceegars, chewing snuff, and likkers of all sorts . . . all of em is intended to make lif a littel more comfertable for you — and they dont contain a ounce of comfort their selfs.

No matter where you are, what you are, what you got, or what you aint got — it looks like you got to bring your own comfort with you if you want to get any comfort —

And the only way you can make comfert for your self is by a given your comfort for other folks.

All I know is what I think, and I dont know that for shore.

But it looks like we ott to have a new system of money destribution.

The way it is a few guys print up all they need and they make the miscalculation of a thinking that's all everybody needs.

I wood favor a system of Money called the Home Money Printing System.

It wood work like this:

Ever Home wood be pervided with a portable Money Makin Machene, with a daily capacity of say $10 — (Carpenters Wages) —

But it woodent run off no more than $10.

Just before breakfast it wood strike — and out wood come $2.50.

Jest before noon it wood strike, an bang out $2.50 more. Same way for dinner (supper in Oklahoma) — $2.50 — and then when nite come, it wood crank out $2.50 more to go out on.

Single folks wood get the same as married folks . . . they waste twice as much as married folks use, any way.

You know, over there at that Trafick Courte, they have your case over with in a bout 5 to 7 minits — an can fine you $10 or $25, or what not, all in from 5 to 7 minits.

Now out here at th Reelief Office, they got a hole houseful of people there a wantin somethin to eat — an they spend ten times as much time an energy, an still dont give you the $25 . . .

I was just a thinkin, the world wood be a steppin out — if you cood just plead hungry or not hungry, an have it all over with, an be on a job, in — 5 to 7 minits.

Billionaires cause hoboes, and hoboes make billionaires. Yet both cuss the other and say they are wrong . . . but personal I ruther trust the hoboes. Most of what I know I learned from the kids and the hoboes.

Kids first. Hoboes second. Rich folks last — and I dont give a dam if you like it or not.

After an original drawing by Woody Guthrie

4 Listen to the kids and the dreamers

Flush — Special to The People's World: Oct. 7. A big, long, tall, husky, loud, noisy 8¼ pound Baby Boy arrived at my house.

Wife has been used to hearing baby girls yeell. Says this one sounds like 3 tribes of Cherokees a havin a Green Corn Dance — some voice.

Been a watchin him mighty close to see if he's a right winger or a left winger. Impossible to keep cover on him. Kicks worse then a millionaire getting taxed 2 cents. Can't quite understand his language, but deciphered this much, "To hell with these baby bottles, an' baby nipples, an baby dresses — bring me a T Bone Steak, a .22 rifle, a walking plow, and a pair of overalls."

Aint thought of no name for him yet. Fact, aint thought since he got here. Dont know what kind of a trip he had, but it must a been a long one. He sleeps all the time. Makes me sleepy to look at him. But I can't sleep. (I'm th' head nursemaid out at our house now.)

He's a Ham & Egger. If things dont go as they ott to, he proceeds to make 7 speeches in 6 difrent languages, all at th same time. Deciphered some more: "Two thirds of me is ill-housed, ill fed, and ill clothed — for goodness sake, TRY SOME-THING!"

Wife is resting nicely — fighting the other 2 kids off of this one. All the credit goes to her.

(The kids laid me out in the first round.) She says give you her regards and — then It broke out with a speech about Low Cost Housing.

I says to the Wife, Okay, I'll write your regards — and then It gurgled out something about me buying him an Airplane.

You know, some people believe in cutting the kid crop down to fit a social system that is two-thirds a failure. I say overhaul the system to make it support the kids, from 1 to 101. Would you throw away your money because of a hole in your pocketbook? No, you'd get you a new pocket-book that would work.

Wife and me has got let's see, two girls, and this Boy — you might say our family is like the Roosevelts, on our Third Time 'Round.

BILL (Woody's 8½ lb. boy) SAYS:

GLENDALE, Oct. 13th. Nice large day. Sun got up in th nice shape. I bet the electric bill on that sun is awful high.

Some fellow come over today to see me, and got $17 off of my old man. They said he was the Landlord. Said he had to charge us for being here. Got a big fence built up around the house. Says the lot belongs to him. Also the house.

Am looking for a Skylord to come over any time and charge us for breathing the air.

Just got a letter from home that says my folks got the album of Dustbowl Ballads I sent them, and that my youngest daughter, Sue, 4, sets and listens to them every day. One record is called, "I'm a Dustbowl Refugee — ." Sue cocks her head over to one side, listens a while, and then goes around over the neighborhood playing and the grandparents hear her singing to herself: "I'm a Dust Storm, I'm a Dust Storm!"

If I know anything worth knowing, or think anything worth thinking or working towards, — about half of it I picked up just by listening to the kids.

Not long ago my little girl, Teeny, she's 3, pulled a mighty good one. You see the landlord was over at our house in Texas puttering around trying to fix up some old rotten boards that was as flimsy as a Roosevelt speech, and he decided that his trouble was termites, or stick tights, or lobby ites, or something, and he said he would like to have a box of some kind of powders to chase them off with. So I took out a quarter and flipped it over to Teeny, and she grabbed it up and skipped off down the driveway, to the store. She was singing some kind of a little song about something or other when she skipped over to the clerk, and throwed her two bits up on the counter and said, My Daddy wants a box of something to get rid of the Landlord.

Aunt Molly Jackson has opened up a Eatin' Joint. Calls it Aunt Molly Jackson's Community Center, 145 Johnson St., corner Duffield St., and Flatbush Ave, Ext, Brooklyn, N.Y. and she Sings while you sip. Her spaghetti has got a marvelous tone, and her soup sounds better than her phonograph, but you can have a good time and gain weight at Aunt Molly's 'cause she feeds you on the basis of 'Vitaphones' — and you can go hungry and gain weight, or eat like a horse and lose your hips — all according to the Vitaphones. Everybody in that neighborhood (which is a highly unorganized section, too) is now a singing Leadbelly's "Borgoise Blues," or "Why Do You Stand There in the Rain" — and I dont know about Aunt Molly, but I cleaned up a small fortune back out west with a cafe that operated in connection with a local clinic — and we — well, between the singing and the food, we got a nice little cut from a nearby clinic. Naw, I'm skidding aside, her eats are swell, and she's just opened up the place, and I know Winchell wont mention her, so I say, for a exasperation inhalation of

groceries, or a superb sip of something, go to Aunt Mollys — Proletarian Potatoes, the best in town.

John Garland says he worked in the Kentucky Coal Mines all of his life, most of his folks died down in there somewhere. He says, "I'm 29 years old. Yep, 29 years old, just right for drafting. I got three kids, two girls and one boy. Hell of a thing. Me twenty-nine. I would have been thirty by rights, but you see, I was awful bad sick one whole year . . . "

Mother Bloor is without a doubt the youngest person I ever seen, cause you see she's done been around and half way back — she's younger than me, because she's that way twice. I aint but once. If I knew setting here looking out into this noisey New York Night that I would be as young and peppy and friendly as Mother Bloor when I have passed that number of summers away — I would be pretty easy to deal with. If I knew that I could use my days to as good an advantage, and my reasons to as fruitful an end, and sow that seeds, and break the good ground, and spread the life and fertility, and bring in the good crops that she has — I would be pretty easy to get along with. I guess she has always looked away far ahead. She must have. She must have done her best with every one of her days, and always kept an eye peeled on the future. She looks like she comes every day upon something she has been hunting for all of her life. That is because she knew what she was hunting for — and what she was planting — and now to wake up every morning, and look all around her every day and see all of this good movement getting hundreds and thousands of times stronger, the day of her hopes and her dreams must be today. Today is the only day she really cares about today. She looks in her eyes like she knows that if you handle today okay, tomorrow will take care of itself. I was told about Mother Bloor by her grand daughter, Herta, in California last summer — and I drew a picture in my mind of the best all around grand-mother I could draw — and Mother Bloor is just exactly That.

Sara Ogan is the wife of a Kentucky Coal Miner. Her man died with T. B., caused by working too long and too hard in the mines. Sara's got 2 of the finest and best children you ever seen. A boy and a girl.

Me and Sara's been a setting around a singing Hill-country Songs, and I swear to goodness she's got one of the best bunches of Original Home Made Songs I ever seen . . . and a dad-gum good honest Kentucky Voice to go along with it.

She snuck in the Jail House through a hole in the rear wall to bring secret notes and letters to Strikers that was in Jail. She went back under the mountain in a big black coal shaft every night and stole a sack of coal to cook meals for her kids and sick husband. She met the sheriff, and he said, "What ya got in that there sack, Sary?" And Sara says, "It's so dark I dont know if it's lumps of coal or rocks, sherf . . . " He says, "You dam shore better'd not let me cetch you a stealin' that coal no more, Sary, I'll throw you in jail shore as hell . . . dont let me cetch you here no more."

"You'll cetch me right here again as quick as the kids get hungry and when I git to a needin' some more coal, Sherf."

The Sherf rode on.

5 Take a look at Skid Row

Skid Row use to be called Skid Road. That
name was started by the lumberjacks. In the little
old towns the board walk that led to the honky
tonks and rooming houses, got awful wet and
slick when it would rain. When you come a
cranking into town with your big hob nail boots
on, and got up on that board walk, it was slicker
than a bankers dream. You had just about the
same chance of standing up as you got to retire at
forty. You skidded up on the boards, you hoisted
your first leg to take a step, and then you got up
out of the mud hole and tried her again. The walk
led down past a little row of ramshackle buildings
and into the only kind of amusement that the
boys knew, just a little flipping of the lid of a pay
day — and back into the timber again to outwork
a team of horses. As bigger towns jumped up,
these working boys, as usual, had to live in the
older, broke down parts of town . . . and it was
still called The Skid Road. Since paved streets
come out, and old dirty greasy slums and dives
and, well, the same old buildings, just 25 years
dirtier, well — the name got to be Skid Row. The
dull lights. The greasy spoons. The flops. The
bucket shops. The "Row." — I'll skid through a
few that I've skidded through:

Los Angeles Skid Row is gray as an overseas
army tent, and slicker than a barrel of slime. It's

really too stinking a subject for a writer to tackle, but I can't make no worse fizzle than the W.P. A. Heads has done. You are standing down there on 5th St., east of Main, and it's so filthy you've got to keep moving your feet, or you'll slip down. No self respecting germ would raise his family there. He might skid down once in a while to see how rotten politics was, but he would stach his wife and family out somewhere at the edge of town. Those old whapperjawed buildings was give up to die fifteen years ago, and they have, but they just aint fell yet. So rent is twice too high. But 10 times too high uptown. So you can eat just twice too high down there, if you can manage to keep from skidding off of the cafe stool, or lick their spoons without vomiting. A bed costs you 20c. 20 men to a room. All snoring so loud it sounds like the magneto line being bombed. In my better days I could sing above the snoring. I hope I still can. When you think of all of the good clean houses and buildings that get bombed to pieces in rich folks's wars, it makes you want to take that money and build a nice, clean, Non Skid Row. For this we're gonna have to elect some Union Non Skid Politicians.

Stockton, Calif., is about as good a place as you can starve to death in. If you ever happen to get stranded there, here's a tip: Go down there back

of that Japanese flop house, called the What Cheer Rooms, and go up the stairs, and down the hall, and turn to your left and you'll hear a voice a singing some kind of a scrap iron chant, then you'll see a big black greasy door, a screen door all clogged up with grease, soot, and meat smoke, and you'll smell, over to your left, a helluva garbage can with a stink like a W. P. A. Cut, and you take the lid off and fight the flies out of your way, and run your arm down into the garbage about a foot, till you find yourself 2 or 3 good soggy, slimey, slices of bread, and you pull it out and wad it up in your hands, till you make a hard ball of dough out of it, and take it over their to the wharf of Stockton, and you can catch you a pretty fair carp there in about an hour. Take this fish back over to the flophouse and he will cook the whole thing, and give you half of it. The other half he will sell for 12c. Just thought I better hand you this recipe till we see how the coming election goes.

But the Skiddiest Row I ever seen is the Bowery in New York City. I didn't know human beings could get so broke, hungry, and so dirty and ragged, and still remain alive. The wine they drink must come out through the pores of their skin and get the disease germs so drunk they can't organize. I slept in lots of the flip flops on the bowery. In Los Angeles they got a flop house called the U. S. Rooms. In New York I stayed in one called the White House Rooms. (Well, that's just about right.) Both cost you 20 cents. Worth about a nickel, if you could talk 'em into putting on some clean bed sheets. Guys passed out drunk on the cement steps of the stores and banks. Draped around the light posts, slumped over the fire plugs, and sleeping around up against the bronze statues in the parks — and any one of them statues cost enough to feed a man a solid year. If you happen to have the notion in your head that there aint no work to be done except to spend all of your money on bombs — I suggest that you take a look at Skid Row and invest your money in making men out of bums.

I WAS DOWN ON SKID ROW AGIN LAST NIGHT. I asked a girl how much she made a playin a guittar in a saloon — an she said she got a doller wages — an then the Kitty — an she said some nightes she made 15c — some nightes 20c an some nightes was purty slow. I asked her how long she plaid — an she said they plaid 7 hours, from 5 to 12. I asked her how long she'd ben a playin on skid row, an she said a bout 2 yrs.

I knew her over a year ago down on 5th St. and I use to drop in to lots of the joints just to sing a song, or extercise my tonsils or drink a bite to eat . . . an you wood be surprised what you cood learn a bout the hole world just by a lookin a round down on Skid Row. An this girl knew more a bout Lost Angeles, then ½ of the fellers that's a runnin it.

If the musiciens was to tell all they know — a bout saloons and parties, an drunks, an fights, an rackets, they wood be 6 jillion deevorces filed tomorrow.

I spent the night in a room with 20 men. It cost 20c. It was worth it to see the 20 men a tryin to find the right bed. Course you caint sleep, not much, but the show is fine. The lihts are turned out — an you got to find youre bed in the dark — an it looked like some beds had 7 fellers in em, an others dident have eny. If one of the fellers come in stewed, an got in th wrong bed, it throwed th whole thing out of order, like a Committee Meetin in Sacramento. (Some platforms has got 6 Candidates a sleepin on em, an other platforms is plumb empty... only they is all ways a good set of coat tails a round the capital to sleep on.)

SKID ROW is generally where you land when you first hit Los Angeles on freight train a blowin out of the Dustbowl.

TWO REASONS why you hit Skid Row is somethin to eat, an somewheres to sleep.

YOU CAN DO BOTH CHEAPER on Skid Row then you can in the more civilised sections of town. Besides the Police bother you too much in the classier sections.

THEY GOT MORE POLICEMEN in the white coller destricts then enywhere else. Well, I guess they need em.

I SOMETIMES THINK OF A POLICEMAN AS A FELLER that wont let you take back what some guy has just took from you.

OTHER TIMES I think the policemen is all right. A feller tole me they pertected the widows an orphens. So you can see they are okay. But they shure gives us hoboes a run for youre money. I shood of said: they run us without the money. An the less money you got, the further they run you.

SKID ROW IS SKID ROW because all of the r.r. hobos is skidded off down there — so's they wont go to sleep on the lawns out on millionair avenew. They got a dog tied out on ever lawn to keep the tramps off. Personal I wood think they ott to hire a tramp to keep the dogs off. But you see people of all opininians.

SO YOU CAN EXPECT QUITE A MIXTURE DOWN ON SKID ROW — an you will get it. Specialy if you buy one of them cheap meals.

You'll get enough weight in the meal to load down a waggon, but not enoufgh newtritian to make a corpussel backfire.

After an original drawing by Woody Guthrie

6 I ain't a gonna kill nobody

Boy, howdy, I'm hottern a sheep at a country fiar, but so is Europe. Todays news is more or less a simple thing. Hitler has done hijacked Poland and is a hollerin peace. Chamberlain is still a talkin. Warsaw has gone done a fightin. Joe Louis is th worlds best boxer. Le Guardia is New Yorks best Mayor. Olsen is Californias best governor. Roosevelt is the USA best bet for 1940. Several folks has clapsed down from the heat waves, an severl others from th radeo waves. Th Western Union boys are on th march. Wall St. is votin th Starvation Ticket. Congress is a meetin to hear FDR speak on neutrition. Prices are still a goin up like a Goodyear blimp. Wages aint so hot. Everybody's a joinin th Union. Horray for everybody. I think I'll go down an join everything.

Hear Woody on the Air daily KFVD USA L.A. 215 to 245 afternoons. . . Notice, You now get a auto graft picture, post card size, with ever copy of Woody's new book $30 Wood Help.

WAR is game played by maniacs who kill each other.

It is murder, studied, prepared and planned by insane minds, and followed by a bunch of thieves.

You can't believe in life, and wear the uniform of death.

There are certain men who never think of any other thing besides slaughter. They are blood soaked butchers and they are believed to be heroes.

Three fifths of the people decide to murder the other two fifths, who must take up killing in order to stay alive.

Locate the man who profits by war and strip him of his profits — war will end.

Rather weed out a few flesh eaters from the race than to see ten nations of people hypnotized to murder, and to run over the rim of the canyon of death and chalked up in Wall Street's banks as so much per carcass.

We feel sorry for the dads, sons, mothers, sweethearts and all of the little kids that are getting bombed in Britain and Germany. We feel just as sorry for one bunch as the other. A kid is a kid and a bomb is a bomb.

As long as the pore folks fights the rich folks wars, you'll keep a havin' pore folks, rich folks, and wars. It's the rich folks thet makes the pore folks; it's the pore folks thet makes the rich folks;

an' it's the two of 'em thet makes wars — rich folks ram-roddin' 'em, an pore folks a fighten' 'em.

Do away with pore folks. Do away with rich folks. Do away with middle class folks. An' you automatically do away with wars.

I wood have a lots of fights if I had a nother feller to fight 'em for me. But since I got to do my own fightin, I try not to have no trouble.

Same way with everbody. Make 'em do there own fightin' — and you do away with fightin.

See where it take 800 pounds of powder to shoot the big 16 inch guns at Fort Tilden, Queens. The bullets just weighs 2,100 lbs. Cost you $3,000. (Yes, I mean YOU.)

That $3,000 would buy a mighty good house and lot for your family to live in for a minimum of 2,100 months and would get you 60,000 pounds of pinto beans, or 2 brand new 1940 automobiles, or send your kid to college.

Just one shot. Even if it's a practice shot. Just one big boom and fancy smoke ring, and whiz goes your dough. You holler, Oh, I didn't have anything to do with all of this waste of time, money, and lives. You did, you voted for the very man that had the power to spend your money for you.

See a picture of the sahary desert in todays paper — but you can't see the sand for the tanks. Won't be long till they (these so called smart guys you voted for) — will be sailing these $3,000 shells, out across the face of the old sahary, and she never produced a hat full of groceries since she's been there.

It looks like 8 folks got throwed in the calaboose just for passing around peace petitions. I reckon they'll go around to all of the doors in the country now and take everybody's fingerprints off of the bells. It's getting easier and easier to get in jail. When it gets down to ringing door bells and getting folks to sign peace petitions — well, the next move will be just to throw you in the jug for believing what ever you believe, makes no difference what it happens to be. So remember I told you, here after you are running a risk to believe anything worth mentioning.

Somebody left the door open in Congress. I feel a Draft. Dam sure better close that door.

Take this Draft Issue. Married men aint got no guarantee against being drafted. Single men are headed down the corral shute that leads to the packing plant of War, where men are made into hamburger meat, young boys into steaks, en-

After an original drawing by Woody Guthrie

gineers into chops, and the college kids into flying, disconnected, disassociated, unrelated, dis-
franchised, dispossessed, worthless, useless,
moneyless, homeless, hunk of human anatomy. I
ruther see these boys, all together, all standing
around talking, working on safe roads, school
houses, hospitals, new factories, good houses. I
wonder who causes these wars? Big rich people,
or did the poor folks just decide all at once to
saddle up and buckle up, and grab up a handful
of shootin' irons, and jump on somebody? That
sounds haywire to me. No, it wasn't them. They
want to work. They don't want to fight. Let me
tell you, Mr. John D. Workingman, War Is Hell, I
know, I got 3 cousins older than me that went
over. One aint used his left arm since, and the
other one sets and spits bloody corruption at
night, yes, ever since 1918, and the third one,
well, you might say that he aint made a dollar
since.

WELL I see where the Chinese and the
Japanese are still at it . . . (expression of
remorse) . . . an' in all probability both of 'em
wood like to be out of it.

Japan may of bit off more'n she can chew — er
did she ever git it bit off?

They got a joke down in South America about the ant thet went over an' stung the ant-eater . . . an' then the ant-eater woke up, an got sore about it, an went over an' et up all of the ants.

That reminds me of China — if Japan keeps on a droppin them bombs around over there, China's gonna come out of the hay like a Brahma Steer — an' I wood say — put up the most surprising fight the civilised countries has seen.

Well, they used to be an old Alabama Boy down where I come from that was good natured, easy satisfied, asked fer very little, dident much care, never put on no show, jest sort of smiled all of the time, in a quiet, easy goin way — an' one afternoon, on th' way home from school, the village "bully" singled this old boy out for some plain and fancy insultin' — an' the old boy jest grinned an' took it . . .

Till after a while they got him started, an' sir, the hair and hide really flew around there for about a hour; and they was bullies, would-be bullies, has-been bullies, an' bully-worshippers — a kickin' up dust in ever direction!

An' — (I aint no prophet) — but, with a equal break, with powder an' shot, I wood not bet 1 red cent that Japan, or 3 more like Japan, cood conquer th' Spirit of the August an' Noble, Peace Worshipping China.

Some war. Seems like theyre a fightin to see who owns who . . . Well if th countery belonged to ever body in it they coodent no fights break out.

Only time you wood see a brawl wood be when some folks tried to fence a county off an call it his.

I under stand a bout a dozen fellers has got Calif. fenced off — boy they are shure some ig-nernt people a runnin loose.

Dear Prof.: I fell in love with a young and handsome boy of twenty-five. 6 feet tall, broad shoulders, deep chest, straight back, a keen mind, a gallant lover, and a true blue pal. Last night I had a dream about him. It happened when he told me that he would like to go to war. I dreamed that I saw him just at sundown, just a shadow holding a gun and a bayonet. Shells ex-ploded everywhere about him. Suddenly a great white flash burst, there was a crack, a roar, and a great hot flame — then a thundering of shrapnel and flying steel. Then I looked for him in the night and he was not to be found. Later I searched the hospitals. There I saw thousands on thousands of bodies almost exactly like him, face-less, eyeless, earless, scared, scalded, ripped and torn beyond recognition, raving, moaning, sob-bing, staring like maniacs . . . their pitiful condition ten hundred times worse than any movie make up man could ever devise. Then I awoke. I never batted a single eye that night. What would you advise me to do?

WONDERING

States back in the east country aint much bigger than back yards out west. When I was in Washington the other day I got up in the morning and walked about a mile down the road, and I covered 2 states, Virginia, and Washington, D.C.

A Taxi Driver says, Say, I'll take you out for a drive through the Arlington Cemetery for a $1.50, that's where the boys are buried that fought in the World War. He headed off down that way without asking me where I was going, and I says, Mister, I don't want to go where the dead folks are. I'd like for you to take me to where the live ones are.

He says, I'll show you the whole thing for $1.50, and I guarantee to show you plenty of dead folks and their graves and their keepsakes, and their wreaths, and their statues, and their monuments, and you aint seen Washington, D. C. till you've seen the graves of the dead soldiers . . . and I thought to myself, Well. I guess their funerals was planned and figured out ahead of time in Washington, but hell, do you have to pay a buck and a half just to see where they buried 'em? That's what I call profiteering on both ends, before and after death.

I took a bath this morning in six war speeches, and a sprinkle of peace. Looks like ever body is declaring war against the forces of force. That's what you get for building up a big war machine. It scares your neighbors into jumping on you, and then of course they them selves have to use force, so you are against their force, and they're aginst yours. Looks like the ring has been drawed and the marbles are all in. The millionaires has throwed their silk hats and our last set of drawers in the ring. The fuse is lit and the cannon is set, and somebody is in for a frailin. I would like to see every single soldier on every single side, just take off your helmet, unbuckle your kit, lay down your rifle, and set down at the side of some shady lane, and say, nope, I aint a gonna kill nobody. Plenty of rich folks wants to fight. Give them the guns.

Well, they tell me they got lands where they will
  not let you stand
In the rain and ask for jobs upon the lawn . . .
Thank God, in the U.S.A., you can stand there all
  the day . . .
But I would not guarantee they'd take you on.

  CHORUS

Why do you stand there in the Rain?
Why do you stand there in the Rain?
These are strange carryings on,
On the White House Capitol lawn,
Tell me Why do you stand there in the Rain?

"Twaddle," the President's voice did ring. Why
  this is the silliest thing
I have heard in all my fifty-eight years of life . . .
But it all just stands to reason, as he passes
  another season,
He'll be smarter by the time he's fifty-nine.

  CHORUS

Now, before the storm could break, Mr. John L.
  Lewis spake,
And he said you asked for jobs, what did you
  get?

And a kid of seventeen who was pretty smart it
   seemed,
Said, we asked them for a job, but we got
   . . . wet.

   CHORUS

Now the guns of Europe roar as they have so oft
   before,
And the warlords play their same old game
   again . . .
While they butcher and they kill, Uncle Sammy
   foots the bill,
With his own dear children standing in the rain.

7 I've been a travelin' on

A TRUE STORY: My wife, the 2 daughters, an' myself — bott a U.S.E.D. car not long ago. It cost us $45 — an' the finance charges, etc., (you know the old story) — run the price up to $61.

The first week we had it, the unusual joint fell out of it. We put in a new outfit.

The battery woodent turn a jumpin' bean over. We bott a new one for $10.

To pour oil in it was jest like a throwin' oil out of the window. It used a quart ever time it backfired, an' 2 quarts when it run front ways.

We all jumped in it an' started down to San Diego . . . We got all most to Oceanside, 93 miles, and it throwed 3 rods around the block, 2 across the street, 9 up on top of a house, 4 thru the engine head, and 1 thru the radiater.

We was stranded. Refugees again. We had to sleep all night in the depot, an' called some friends over the phone wires, to come an' get us.

I told the Car Co. where the wreck was — an' to go and git it. They went down an' got it. Re-sold it again for $45. An' sent me a bill for $6.

I sed I'm a runnin for governor on the Chinese Laundry Ticket, and when I git elected I'll pay you the $6.

SHUCKS I dident know they was so much pay off to a gallon of gas.

Just a grazin over th papers here it says they got a divvy den, i mean a divvy den pay off, a over head pay off, a under hand pay off, a advertisin pay off, an you got ploticians to pay off an keep paid off, an they pay em off again — an a leggal pay off, an a lobby pay off, an a bunch of other pay offs — .

I thought my car was a heavin a little when i left home this mornin — sorta humped up, an bucked up when I started up a hill — an I figgered I wood drive over an bawl out th guy I bouht it from.

But you know, after I got wise to what all was a goin on in its gas tank, I says to myself, I don't blame it for a kickin.

I am putting forth another scientific observation — which came along after several years of hard study — 'In my opinion, no two automobiles can occupy the same space at the same time.' Although this has been tried over and over many, many times — it has brought considerable damage to the automobiles — sometimes making them completely unfit for use.

There are a number of names that I have given to different kinds of drivers, and in the interest of Safe Driving, I give them here: 1st, is what is

known as a "middle-buster," a driver who strad-
dles the white line, and chooses his half of the
road out of the middle, and makes it dangerous
and bad on 17,000 other cars beside himself on
the highways.

2nd, is what you wood call a "Light Rusher" —
this is a driver that sails into the road crossing
between the bells — and scares the wits out of
12,000 other drivers who are also trying to get
around.

3rd, you see what you call a "Line Slider," who
always drives 35 m.p.h. up to a stop light, and
then throws on his brakes, and slides about six
feet across the line where 11,000 folks are trying
to walk across the street. He james up a couple of
hunderd cars behind him, that many in front of
him, and completely bumfuzzles that many coming in off of the side streets.

4th, you see the "Safety Zone Zoomers" — he
zoomes through all of the safety zones where
13,000 folks are trying to catch street cars — and
forces them to make a ten foot dive into the street
cars — or a 12 ft. dive onto the curb. He also
always manages to park with at least one wheel
in the safety zone . . . and crowds the sisters up
the street lights and chases the kids up onto the
mail boxes, or upon a fire plug.

5th, you see the "Bullfrog Leapers" — who, in order to show you how good they can drive, and how fast their car will get away, give it all the gas at the go sign and leap entirely across the street — generally over a couple of street cars, and a garbage truck or two.

6th, you see what's called the "Side-winder" — a driver who does not know which side of the road he wants, and therefore winds constantly from side to side — trying them both out, at the same time driving so slow that you want to pass him, but wide winding so much that 18,000 trucks and cars must drive 4 hours in order to travel 6 blocks.

7th, the "Jalloppie Popper" — is the young driver that turns his switch off and on in the tunnel and on the streets — so as to hear his Jalloppie backfire like a hand grenade — usually, causing from 3 to 7 nervous wrecks at very close range.

No doubt there are others — my time is so limited that I cant cover them all — there's the "Part Slinger," the "Curb Skidder," "College Creeper," "High School Hopper," "High Rollers," "Easy Riders," and you see signs on lots of them that say "No Riders" — they ought to be truthful about it, and put up a sign saying, No Driver.

A feller by the name of Renfro lives out clost to me. He's in th USED tire business. He says business is rotten. I bet the tires aint no rottener then the cafe business.

Renfro drives a big Nash, a puritan model with Hollywood tendencies — an I catch a ride with him most everywhere I go. He said the tires still held him up. He says the new tire dealers hold you up best.

I had a Grahem-Cracker Page, 6 sylinders, 3 of em never been used, an it had a split in the conservative bloc — an all of the spark plugs voted a different ticket — an when the battery fired 2 of em, the other 4 wood strike, an the lobbyist rings (rings) pumped more oil then Huntinton Beach cood perduce . . . I was purty well satisfied with the performance, but not with the traporstation — it was more of a comedy then a car. I was glad it come a part — afrade some of the gears wood fly off an hit the kids.

Just got a look at a string of cars lining up and down the highway for 100 miles in each direction. Week enders here in New York. I never seen the like. If the highways get any more crowded, you'll have to take your vacation on the other end. THE NEW YORKIES out-migrate the Oakies of a week end. But the highways are so crowded, the Oakies make the best time.

I know one feller that takes a hoe and rake and a small cultivator along with him when he drives on the New York highway. I asked him what he done that for. He said it was so crowded, you went so slow, that he was aiming to put in a crop of late corn along side the road.

ST LOUIS, Mo. — Birds a-singing this morning and not a soldier in sight. All clear and bright, not a bomb a-falling. It's so quiet here in Virginia that you can hear the stillness — or maybe — what is that you can hear? Devil of a note . . . let me go over here and see what that is. No, it ain't the Stillness, it's the Still. Gave a 65-year-old lady a ride last night over the Blue Ridge Mountains, and she said she'd been a-sleeping out by the side of the road. She says, Where you Boys a-Goin'? We said, Just up here in the Mountains. She says, What Mountains? We says, Oh, just any that come handy. She says, What you goin' fer? We said, Oh, just to look the Mountains over — Hmmmmm, she said, You can just stop this car and let me out right here, just stop and let me out. And we tried to get her to ride up to the next town, but nosiree, she wasn't going to, — she got out away out there 15 miles from nowhere, and I cant see to my soul why she done it. Probably thought we was cops. In that case, I don't blame her for not riding with us. Gonna buy me a badge that says, Notice, I Aint a Cop, I'm just a Feller.

FORT SMITH, Ark. — Dont know what day it is. Cant find any body else that knows what year it is. Some think the calendar is going backwards. Judging from these rich folks wars, civilization is going that a way. Met some nice friends last night, but the names I forget. They read the Daily Worker. To heck with names, I know they're friends. Oh yes, we're arranging that Victor Album into order, playing the test records and writing down the mistakes, and there was so many mistakes per record that they was having some trouble about it, and I said, shucks, fellers, them mistakes is what will make the album, makes it "homey" — and I held out for more money. I want to apologize for leaving New York and all of you folks that I had dates will just have to be patient till I can get a little further away. Guess you like this green spring weather as good as I do, and if you do, you just cant help a wanting to inhale as much of it as you can. The climate is mighty good here.

Twenty-five of us one night down on the Mexican Border, whistling out of El Paso, Texas, over the mountains, acrost the flats, and down across the mesas, and the wind was as cold as ice, and the train was making 50. And you know them cattle cars aint got near the heating machinery that a pent house has. Well sir, we dern near froze. We got so cold we had to get up and walk and trot back and forth in the manure on the floor to keep from freezing stiff as a Fifth Ave. face. So we run till we give out, and had to rest. Then we got stiff again. If we started a fire in the cattle car, they'd throw us in jail. So we all commenced to huddle around like a herd of sheep. We would set down. Like this, you would set down, and some body would set down in your lap, and some body in his lap, and some body in his lap, till we formed a big ring, every body setting in every body's lap. You didn't know who's. You couldn't see who's. You dam sure didn't care who's. You was just a grappling there in the dark — but there's a warm heat about a live human being that you are mighty thankful for when you've been out in the cold so long.

Boy I been a going through the states almost fast as a WPA Cut — an that's dam fast. Two carloads of us Oakies come up for the convention. Thirteen of us. Drove night and day. Wore out 3 watches and 2 alarm clocks trying to keep up with that new fangled daylight saving time . . . some towns got it, some towns aint, you know, just like organization. Some towns got it, some towns aint,some towns can, some towns cant, some towns will, some towns wont, some towns do, some towns dont, some towns could, some towns couldnt, some towns should, no town shouldnt, big towns want to, little towns need to, middle towns got to, hick towns fixing to — but rip, ravel or bust, every every town's GOT to.

A lot of folks in our caravan was a coming to New York for their first time. After we got out of the Holler Tunnel, I says, Well, Boys, what do you think of her? One old boy in the back said, I bet I sunburn the roof of my mouth — but it'll be worth it — he looked out the window as we drove down the street and he said, God a mighty, dadburn my hide, is ALL of them people here for the Convention? — Another ol boy said, Well, yeah, but they just dont KNOW IT yet.

ROVING REPORTER COVERS HUNGER BY A DAM SITE; JUST 'A FREE SOUL LOOKIN FER A FREE MEAL'

They was a little talk about a big dam to be built up at Redding, Calif. That was a long time ago. So I hung a fast freight an breezed right on into Redding jest to see how they perceeded to git the workers an' build a dam.

Well the dam job had been set an postponed about 14 times — an each time from 10 to 90 days.

An ever day droves an droves of fellers was a fallin off of the freight trains to build the dam.

Well, they was about 7000 men got there about 60 days ahead of time.

(I think the board of directors was a tryin to decide on some kodak pictures of the dam site.) (So it was put off and put off.)

An the would be workers worked harder a tryin to keep from starvin in the jungles then if they had built 2 dams.

You might say they was hungry by a dam site. An I lived right out in the tall timber with em — an et an drunk out of ole smokey tin cans an slep without no cover — an, well, we jest was a givin the coyotes lessons in outdoor livin.

You was lucky to get one meal a day. Most of the boys was flat busted. Hit town with $5 or $10 which dont last long in a dam boom.

The men was riveters, jack hammers, powder monkeys, welders, mechanics, tractor drivers, bull dozers, cement masons, mixers, an crane an shovel operators. An lots of em had worked on other big dams around over the country.

An I jest sorta blundered around ever day to get some idees of what kind of life these builders of our civilization lead.

Well I got a dadgum good idee — and I got a lot of other good idees too.

The saloons an gamblin halls an unfamous hotels was all operatin very nicely. I belive that ever time the ploticians an gamblers an likker dealers had a misunderstanden — why, they delayed the dam job another 2 weeks.

Ever body thot that money wood be knee deep when the dam started but they all had a hard time a gettin fixed for it.

I bet they was more palms decorated among the ploticians then they was blistered among the workers.

(They is more honor in a blistered palm then a decorated one.)

Where was I at? Oh yes, a runnin down the ploticians.

They had about 46 7–8 crooked card games a going on one street. With 14 crooked dealers an 9 house men in ever game.

They worked harder a friskin the worker than

the worker did a buildin the dam. Or is it built yet? I ott to of said they frisked the worker before he cood get a dam job.

If Redding had gone at that rate very far — very long — it wood soon of been as slummy as Sacramentoe. Or 5th & Main in L.A. Boy Howdy! An you got to really get unsanitary to beat that.

They was more people on relief than they was people who lived in Redding.

When a hobo (noble worker) got a good feed at a house he just painted a big X on the gate or door or house — an they was so many bo's hustlin grub that ever house in town except the deacon's got 4 X's all over the three trunks.

The homeless brothers of the working game held a special session in the jungles and decided to henceforth mark henhouses only.

(The reason why the preachers house dident git painted was because he never fed nobody.)

It was right entertainin to see the boys an to see how they live.

Communin' with mama nature — asleep in the deep (grass) — a free soul — (lookin fer a free meal).

Yes sir — to see em shave an warsh dishes in the spring of water — an then to see another bunch come down an drink it — an another bunch use it for sewage disposal, it was right educational.

It makes you think, most folks dont think they jest sorta coast.

But in the jungles — you think.

Whole families was out in the woods — down on the river, up on some little hills — under the rail road trustles — a livin in houses of a mickey mouse description — made out of junk tin, flattened out buckets, pasteboard boxes, shippin crates, apple boxes, old boilers, etc. (an them that was not so lucky lived jest rudely, crudely, almost nudely).

Women was on the bum — follerin their husbands faithfully into the hobo jungles, bringing little kids an' little babies with em to — find work.

Flies was thicker than lobbyists in the Capitol but not as filthy.

Rattlesnakes was so numerous but less poisonous than a reactionary Senator.

Wives an mothers worked an toiled an sweated an — thank Heaven — even laughed an sung songs around their private fires at nite.

You cood hear them laugh and talk. You cood see little ragged kids run an play. An you cood smell some kind of salty steam from the old an smokey stewpot on the fire. It was breakfast luncheon and dinner. Breakfast dinner an supper to you.

My spaice dont alow me to an neither does my ignorance, to discuss the medicale care and attention of these — my people — nor the parent teacher's meetings — nor the laidies lemonade society — nor the afternoon tea association — nor the pool hall an bowlin news.

When you get to where you perduce for USE instead of for a silly PROFIT — you'll have a cinch on 3 squares a day, an a job — an outside of that I don't know anything about anything.

WOODY

P.S. Oncet more I have accomplished the feat of a gettin off of the subject 17 times in 21 paragrafts — a gettin off of the subject 17 times in 21 paragrafts —

But I seen this with my own eyes an wrote it up the best I cood.

If you dont quite savvy it, catch a Portland bound freight and go see for yore self.

OKLAHOMA CITY, Okla. — Got here today. That's how come us here. Pete's asleep. He's my buddy, sings tenor, using the left tonsil. I see a big crowd down on the streets, just come through it, and this is the day the Food Stamp plan starts. The Workers Alliance has been working like the dickens to get this plan for a mighty long time. One thousand folks will get to eat today, by the looks of their faces, I'd say it will be a new venture for a lot of them. Oklahoma City and Tulsa has got the Plan, and next thing is to try like the devil to get it for all of the other counties, you can get just as hungry there as you can in Tulsa or Oklahoma City. Wish I had a kodak I'd show you some faces and some folks that Steinbeck missed, but I guess he purty well covered all of the hungry folks in the world when he called them just the Joads. This stamp plan gives them 200 per cent more eats than they use to have . . . you know how much 200 per cent is — regular Finance Charges.

OKLAHOMA CITY, Okla. — Come a big rain last night and that was the first nite I was here. Slipped off to a good start. We'd been a needing rain for 7 years, all it's got to do now is rain 75,658 more days in a row, and repeal our prohibition law, wash out the capitol offices, flood the Senators with protests, and a real mudslinging campaign will be under [way]. Heard a joke about a man down close to the Texas Line that fainted when this rain came up after 7 years dry weather, and his wife and two girls had to carry 6 buckets of sand and throw it in his face to bring him back again. But you know it can come a rain down here in the morning and 2 good dust storms before night, and three head rises on the river, and a cyclone chase you home, and lightning strike on the way. Oklahoma has got a lot of Lightning and Thunder, and I guess the reason I like it so good down here is the way it Strikes. Lightning is one of the strongest things in nature, and when you run it Short it really Strikes.

Visited Oklahoma City's "Community Camp" today. You never seen the half of it in "Grapes of Wrath" — because the worst "thing they" showed in the picture was twice as nice as Community Camp.

Met a preacher down the camp that wanted to preach about the war but didn't have a car to go around in nor no singers to draw him a crowd. Said the war was forecast in the Bible and was BOUND to come, right, ravel or bust. We said, What do you reckon caused this war. He said, why the DEVIL caused it.

We said that's right, boy, but WHO is a working with the devil — ?

And he said. It's th' RICH FOLKS. They start all of the wars — and then yell for us poor folks to come do their dyin' for them.

All I got is Community Camp, a $7 house an a dry sandy river bed, alongside a garbage dump — I wouldn't fight for THAT.

These raddio interpretators have it easy goin cause nobody takes the trouble to compare what they say today with what they said yestiday. Like it happened to a friend of mine who had a job on a paper in Oklahoma onct. The head man told him fer to fix a tellygram up fer a big artikel and my friend said we caint do that because the paper said jest the opposite yesterday. Oh thats okay, said the head man, we'd be in a helluva fix if our readers remembered what we wrote yesteday.

How would you like to help me throw a party for Oklahoma? Lordy knows that I appreciate the money and the help and the attention that has been given to the Oakies out in California and now it is evident that good old wind blown, banker bit Oklahoma has been overlooked just a shade in this respect. Bob Wood was up here some time ago and he made some good speeches and raised quite a collection of good clothes and money, but still Oklahoma hasn't got a tank of

SUNDOWN

SUNUP

THIS IS A
DAY

HAND BAWLS WIFE OUT!

WIFE BAWLS HAND OUT!

HAND
CUSSES
BOSS
OUT

BOSS YELLS
COPS

LAW &
ORDER COMES

HAND IS CHARGED WITH TRYING TO
OVERTHROW U.S. GOVERNMENT !

HAND
THINKS
IT OVER

gasoline to go to the little halls and schools and organize the hungry farmers. Raids have been thick lately and Otis Nation, organizer for the Oklahoma Tenant Farmer's Union, got in jail not long ago. I dont know if he's out yet. (Howdy, Otis.) — I'd like to throw a real good party every month for Oklahoma. If you are an entertainer and would give your services any night to Oklahoma, write me a letter, and you'll get on the program. Will you mail out 100 postal cards? Pass out a few handbills? Could you peddle a dozen tickets at 49c a peace? (Even though Peace is against the law these days) — Write your letter to me today so's I'll get it by tomorrow or next day. Exact time and place of Oklahoma's Party will be announced right away. (Planning on a calling it a 'Rapes of Graft Party' — or, some such similar name. Gonna ride herd on all of you entertainers, and we'll have more good left handed singers, dancers, yodelers, fence jumpers, bulldoggers, artists, speakers, geetar thumpers, wild cow milkers, organizers, hoss traders, union preachers, fox trotters, two steppers, deep thinkers, beer drinkers, and American Citizens present than you can shake an afidavit at. Haul off and write to me right now and tell me what you'll do to help Oklahoma. If you're a thinking about me, forget about me and think about Oklahoma.

We just figgered out what it would take for us to throw this party, and it come to $27.65. Boy. That's dern near it as much as the cost of a new battle ship. The committee is dickering. No, wait, we're going ahead with the singing, to heck with the battle ship. Outlaw songs on toast. Standing In The Rain with macaroni. Lead Belly singing the Bushwah Blues with sautern. Come on up.

NEW YORK. — I'm a stranger round here. Could you tell me where the United States is located?

New York is a good town well done. It is a big pile of bricks surrounded by water. I am about to decide on the water. But they got more poor fish here in the city.

A good clean desert has got some good points, and the more I chase around in this streamiline ant hill, the more I think the desert was right.

I like the land. I like the row crop and the wheat fields and the forty acre tracks, where you can holler and yell and sing anyplace in the world, if only it was a little different.

New York is the one and only New York, and I would be a dumb bell to cuss it or call it a big, cold, dark, crowded, nervous, greedy, hurried, lonesome, rat trap — so I will call it the greatest place in the world, if only it was a little different.

I mean if the money and jobs and the good whiskey and women and cars and men and mice were a little bit better distributed.

In a passin out the money, they come to some doors twice every hour, and other doors once a month. Other doors never. Hell, I ain't even got a door.

Here in New York they got the highest building in the world. Call it the Empire State Building. Hundred and ten stories up off the ground. Thousand and ten feet, I think.

You get up there and look off and the world looks like a head of cabbage.

You could jump at Oklahoma City and hit within walkin' distance.

More folks work in this building than they got in some towns. Run elevators and work in offices. And others get the money.

Costs you a dollar bill to go to the top. Elevators really run you down fast. We dropt 34 floors before I could call out my number. That's fast droppin'. Almost dropt as fast as wages.

After we hit bottom my pants kept on a goin'. It never was this a-way back home.

However there are 7,000,000 people here in

New York. I would judge 6,000,000 of 'em has already lost their pants.

Talking about the sky, here in New York you have got to give the taxi company 35 cents cash to get a cab driver to chase some down for you. That's the Capitalist cistern for you, they build up so much buildins to beat you out of money with, that they finally block out the sky, and charge you 20 cts. a mile to ride a round and look at it.

Texas Hamburgers are the world's best. Every other state tries to imitate 'em but you caint do it, less you put the stuff on 'em. I went into a cafe the other night and ordered a 'burger, and the cheff fanned the air with a kitchen tool, slammed and banged a couple of times on the smasher, zipped over the griddle with the bun and meat and then laid 'em up in front of me. Just the bun and just the meat, dont go to imaniging things. Well, I set there and thought he would go ahead and make the hamburger after a while, and put the pickles, onions, mustard, relish, celery, and salt and pepper on it . . . so I just set there. Purty soon he looked up and says, Are you the man that ordered the 'burger? And I says, yep, is it here in the place? And he say's — that's a hamburger right under your nose, and I didn't even know it.

New York is funny. The streets are half a block long and three blocks wide, and the town is half a town wide, and three towns high.

Boy, it really takes the nickels to live here. You can't get to first base unless you make 847446 fone calls, and take 85756 busses every day. You got to spend sixty cents in nickels to see about a dollar job. Then you got to spend the rest of the dollar to get to the right place at the right time.

I believe there is more of New York underground than on top.

They could have more people in these subway trains if they'd lay 'em down. When you got to your station they could shoot you home like a torpedo.

The 5 o'clock trains was so crowded today you couldn't even fall down. I changed stations twice and both times I come out with a different pair of shoes on.

Advice to Peanut Eaters in Subways: If by some slip of fate you happen to put a penny in one of those peanut machines, and by another slip of fate, you accidentally get some peanuts, just phone the slot machine company and they'll send a man down to sling a wrench into it.

I'm still a ramblin' 'round old New York trying to find me a job of work. I been here for about three weeks a walkin' around these old cold streets. Sometimes up and sometimes down, sometimes lost in a hole in the ground.

Seems like two or three times a day I get lost down in the old subway. Electric train comes down the line. I catch out wrong most every time.

One runs east, two go west, and I wonder how to catch on best. Six go south, and nine run north, and you dang sure get your nickels worth.

You put a nickel in the slot and grab you a train that's good and hot, sail out down a hole in the ground and ride that train across this town.

People push and people jam, the jammedest jam I mean what am. You walk, you nudge and squirm and fall, and get up against that cement wall, and ooze and duck and spar and strain and they shove you into the wrong dam train.

Friend told me he run an ad in the Times for a job of work. Run it 4 days and got 4 letters. Three of 'em asked him for a job, and here is the fourth one:

Mr. R. L., N.Y.C., Dear Mr. L., Your application and letter received. I am afraid you have very little to offer, and only one reference that I am sure would be in your favor. The reason I am writing you is that I like your picture. I feel that you would fit in somewhere around our resort. But you would only be paid $50 per month, $40 of this will be for your room and bd., you will receive $10 cash. If this is acceptable, please let me know on this letter. Return your answer by return mail. J., Windham, N.Y.

To which we got together, the job hunter, and me, and wrote back this answer: J., Windham, N.Y., Dear Old Boy, good old J., "Your letter received and contents smelled. I am afraid you have got very little to offer and only one reference that would be in your favor. That is the $50. As for the $40 room and bd., I could bring a hamburger along with me and bd outside. Yet, I'm sure I would fit in somewhere around your resort, as I am an old experienced resort fitter-inner, but you perhaps missed the point of my ad, as I am a professional resort fitter . . . and usually draw about $50 a week. You see I happen to be the only man in America with a face and figure rugged enough to match the landscape proper. I got so good in my younger days that you couldn't tell where my face quit and the trees commenced. But of course I'm 26 now and too old to hold down a good job anymore, judging from the tone of your letter. Say J., if you've got a good suitable creek there handy, I wish you would take a flying high dive and see how good you fit into it. Love and Kisses. Mr. R. L., N.Y. P.S. Hold the phone.

Went into the 42nd Street Library yesterday cause I had a date with a friend (lady) but it began to rain and I went in to keep dry and so afell to readin books. When I was aminded to leave I got held up just before the egress by a turnstile like they have 'em in the subway and a gent — gentlelike but firm — goes through my carry-all to see that I didn't take the Encyclopedia Britannica with me. He shook and shook but all that kum out was a couple of old shirts that I've been atryin to get vulcanized, the financial section of last Monday's Times (want-ads) and three second-hand pretzels that I got at a bar downtown and fergot to use up. The Library attendance officer was satisfied I wasn't tryin to read ennythin and said I could go back home to my folks.

I bought a fountain pen today — the pawn shop feller said it was a "lifetime" pen. Well, judgin from the wars thats a breakin out, a penny pencil will last a lifetime.

Went out to Bronx Park Zoo today. Seen everything you could imagine. Sundays are crowded, and I had a heck of a time a telling where the women's coats stopped and the animals commenced. On one particular occasion I was trying to feed a senator's wife peanuts, and on another one I was throwing herring to a lady in a sealskin.

I started out walking tonight on E. 4th Street and outrun the bus up to 52nd. When I was at a Bus Stop they wasn't a bus in sight, and then when I got in the middle of the dern block, why nine busses, three fire wagons, and six bycicles would sail past. A kiddy car would drive up to the curb and 19 policemen jump out. It was about midnight, and the heaviest traffic was girls on roller skates. I was treed up 4 lamp poles by yellow cabs, and missed the only bus that stopped in my zone. I tanked up on coffee at every joint I come to. When I left 4th Street I was a drinking my supper coffee, and by the time I hit 52nd, it was my breakfast. This same process has been my life, on a coast to coast scale, and I have been an eye witness to the 300,000 other families that are out on the roads a doing this same thing, only it's jobs instead of busses, they're a chasing, and under the present setup they've got just about as much of a chance to grab one as I have of finding my way around in New York City.

Ended up about five o'clock in the mornin' down in Chinatown with a bowl of Chow Main. He said it was Chow Main. It tasted a lot like Horses Main. You know what Chow Main is, don't you? It's a plain, ordinary old 'haystack' just before it goes to the bad.

Sun up in New York. Only trouble is you can't see it. Got to wait till 1:30 p.m. in the afternoon and then it is visible for seven minutes between the Empire State Building and that shoe sign.

No wonder astronomy is a good hobby; even the sunshine has got to be studied for years before these big city folks would recognize it. They read astrology too. They pretend to be interested in fortune telling, but you can't fool me, they're just a fishin' for the sun.

Asphalt's so hot on Sixth Ave. trucks bog down in it worse than a hog wallow. Tar sticks to your shoes when you go over glass things in front of the department stores. But, no use to bellyache dont reckon, the Rich Guys no more than get a good set of roads build up to get run over on, than they commence a war and blow the thing up.

I'd ruther stay over here and get stuck in the tar than to go to war and get stuck with a bayonet. I think the hot weather will have a big effect on the Yanks Not A Comin' — reason why is 'cause they'll be so stuck up in these asphalt streets that they can't get away.

New York's gonna be hotter than a depot stove, I can see that. Winter is gone and summer drawers on. I see a woman out across yonder in the window of a big high building. She's a working in a laundry, pressing all kinds of clothes on a big machine of some kind that looks like its got her chained to it. Nothing wrong with hard work. Nothing wrong with hot work. Nothing wrong with the laundry. Nothing wrong with the woman. But — you dont make enough money to take a vacation and get away from the outfit, that's what's wrong, you got to stand there and stand there, and by George, keep on a standing there till you might as well of been an old machine of some kind when you was born. When I was younger I saw that my bosses wouldn't pay me right. So I lit out down the road when hot weather come, and laid in the shade of trees and went hungry and half naked and half mad — and I could see them big cool cars zip down the road past me, and I'd roll over and watch 'em sail.

Then I'd get to wondering if I really wanted to sing to 'em or shoot at 'em, or just keep on a being a hobo. It's better to work like the lady in the laundry, if you get enough money to be a first class hobo when you get your work done.

They's one thing about New York and that is the way you kin get tomorrow's paper last night, that is tonight. The capitalist papers are so far ahead of the news that they know tonight what happened tomorrow, but they never do go to the trouble of informin' their readers about what they really knew yesterday.

I wore out a pair of new moccasins last night achasin' around the Times Square newspaper building atryin' to kech up on the news. Run around about forty times afollowin' the electric sign to get the end of the disspach but jest then I seen a poleece car and decided it wood be the better part of valor if not comfort ef I went home and read yesterday's paper.

New York is a big town for painting pictures. Least, they call em pictures. Some of em look like you didn't get done with em.

Call em modern paintings. But I'm glad to see

em in fashion. It makes everybody a artist. I mean when you can't get no other kind of a job; why you get a hold of you some paint and you're a artist.

I always did think that all of us was good for something — and now I see what it is. We're painters.

And if you can't tell what our pictures are sposed to be, we take down the $5 tag and put up a $50 one.

Paint — splatters on!

Union Square. 20 men sprawled around asleep at the foot of a statue that says they are blessed with a bunch of things. One bunch of folks talking a language I didn't under stand. However they looked just as broke as me. Another bunch talking about the banking situation. What they got to bank? Another bunch yelling their heads off about Soviet Russia. I never was there. They said they had something to eat over there. Well, it's a long swim. Here's a lot of people chewing the rag about religion. That's all there is to chew. One feller said he didn't believe in nothing except in what was right. Two men looking in each other's ears, eyes, and throats, looking for the holy ghost. Bet they'd jump at a holy roast.

There is one and only one New York, and if you dont see it, you are doing yourself and your country an injustice, it's got the best of the least for the most, and the most of the best for the least, and the biggest bunch of people on earth that work like dogs for a living, and the biggest bunch that live a hole lifetime and never hit a lick of work. Goodbye to New York City. You was a big town before I come along.

WASHINGTON. — Got lost in the halls of the Department of Interior. I dont know what that means. I spose its a bunch of decorators. Decorate the mahogany.

Boy they got buildins here with more buildins inside of em. They build up a buildin and then when it is so old its about to fall down they pitch in and build a marble one around it to hold it up.

Old stuff is awful valuable up here. They have a lot of parties up here. First part of every party is spent a talkin about the last one, and the last half is spent talkin about the next one.

Spies invite other spies to come over to a party and spy on them so the first spy will invite you to come over someday and spy on him.

It has got to all be done polite, but I suppose they know what they're a doing.

If you don't think the Bill of Rights and the Constitution is fading out just go to Washington and look, they had to wax 'em and put 'em behind a big thick glass . . . to keep 'em from goin' plumb blank . . . however, I suppose they get a copy around there in the Congressional Library somewhere. . . .

WASHINGTON, D.C. — Broke this morning, aint got a dime. Everybody hits a little hard luck sometime. Boy, when I just sit here and imagine how much money they got in the world I just wonder how everybody's got to be broke. Windy as the dickens where I'm a writing this morning, so dont get excited if I blow a little. I guess there's plenty of stuff here in Washington that they never air. Oh, well, read the Daily Worker, you'll get wind of it. Woman and a dog a going across the grass. Dont know which is leading. Woman wanted to stop but the dog wouldn't let her. I think maybe she checks that dogs blood pressure before she votes, and then hires three doctors to check up again to see if the election went to suit the pooch. Looking for Leadbelly in town today. He's gonna sing at the Cafe Society here in Washington for Spanish refugees. He bought him a big 12 string guitar, best I ever heard, boy I

can set and listen to him sing Borgoises Blues all
night —

Now all you Colored People listen to me,
Dont you rent no house in Washington Dee Cee,
'Cause it's a Bushwa Town — OOOooooo
It's a Bushwa Town —
It's a Bushwa Town I'm gonna spread the News
    All around.

    In going over the nation's cash account I find
that there aint no cash account to go over.

    I thought the people was suppose to have the
say so over money. But the boys up in the big
offices has fixed it so's you aint got no more say
so over your money than a dead man.

    A little hand full of fellers has stepped in and
carried off all of the money, and now they say
there aint no money to argue about. They got it
off of you, that's something to remind them of.

    I say that if the fellers we elect don't want to
keep their promises and get us jobs and
groceries, I say we make a law to take back all of
the salary and hush money that they make while
they are a holding office.

Coming out of a Theatre Entrance the other night I saw a Chorus Girl readjusting the hamstring on her hose.

On getting up, I descovered that I had run into a telaphone post and was very upset . . . and bashful . . . as a whole big crowd was gathering and lauffing at me.

One nite I dropped off a freight train in the town of Tracy, Calif., and the cops run about 50 of us out in a cow pasture 'cause they caught us a sleepin on a pile of warm sand in a boiler house by the railroad tracks. It was cold an a rainin out there in that pasture so 3 of us sneaked back into town. Cops had bawled us out an told us not to come back to town. And they spotted us with a big search light and that was the second time. They drove us out of town again. A walkin along in front of th' patrol car in th rain. We found some old wet papers and slep under a bridge.

Accused of us of vacancy. Hell, half of th' houses in town said 'vacancy' on em.

WELL, I JUST DONE SOMETHIN I NEVER DONE BEFORE. I MADE HOLLERWOOD

BOLEVARD AN SKID ROW BOTH IN ONE NIGHT.

Say, if you senaters caint find no jobs I tell you what you cood do — we cood pitch in an all go to remodlin Skid Row, an make it stream fine like Hollerwood Bvd.

If they aint but ten jillion folks out of work, I cood put more then that to woark a rakin up leaves.

It aint fair to do all of th work on th classy bvds. an just skip th others. You guys spend all youre time a taxin th folks thet caint stand it an a bildin th streets that dont need it.

All I know a bout Los Angelese is what I learnt a missin busses — and I allready know enoufgh to put 7 nations to work a cleaning up th one we got. . . .

A senater that caint see no work to do caint see nothin.

I woodent recall em for a bein crooks, but I wood for a bein blind.

You guys just pass a bunch of laws that ever street in town has got to look as good as Hollerwood Bvd.

CALIFORNIA IS A PLACE SET ASIDE where you can come out and wrastle with life, grapple for groceries, preach for popcorn, pray for perfume, and punch for pensions.

KANSAS IS A PLACE where you can blow 47 miles out in a cowpasture, and blow 25 more miles acrost the fields, and not see a cow, nor a crop in the whole blow.

TEXAS IS WHERE you can see further, see less, walk farther and travel less, see more cows and less milk, more trees and less shade, more rivers and less water, more fun on less money than anywhere else.

OKLAHOMA IS WHERE you can see miners going down in the hole, oil well drillers going down in the hole, and farmers going into the hole — to get what ever they need. In this respect Oklahoma is just like the rest of the world. You got to go in the hole to get what you need.

After an original drawing by Woody Guthrie

8 That tune told his story

This is what you wood call the age of talent.

The development of yore talent is the mainest thing now days.

You got to develop it to stay in the deal — an after you develop it — well you don't get much for it.

Littel boys an girls use to learn how to play the pianer or blow a horn or pick a guitar or dance — and they was opening for talented folks 'cause they was needed all most ever wheres.

But electric fonagrafts an radeos an talkies has fixed it to where you put a nickel in an — one or 2 musicians entertains hunderds an thousands of people, an hole armies of well talented folks goes a beggin.

Use to be when a musician walked in a saloon he was cinched to make a good stake, 'cause he was welcome.

Now days the bartender says "no music wanted — we got Bang Crosby right over there on the electric fonograft — " an the crowd roars. An the musician sleeps under a bridge.

Same way with art an poetry an dancin' an ever thing else. One or two perferred folks get on the screen or on wax or on the air — and hole flocks go without.

How many fonograft records do the radeo stations use? All most all you here is recorded.

We may be a hole lot more educated but we're jest as hungery as ever.

Okay, you guys, here I come. It looks like everybody in New York has wrote a book, so I'm writing one. I don't know the name of it, and really dont know what the story is — that's what I've got to figure out after I get it wrote down — I got about 300 pages of double space scrip — and it tells about every place I ever been, folks I knew, places I bummed around, jails I got in, back doors I hit, skid rows I played music on, high dives I dove in, flops I slept in, bed bugs I knew by their maiden names — gold mines we chased, fights that we had on election day, and teams of horses that run away, and kids that built gang houses and had their own social system, how one feller made a gambling wheel out of a bicycle wheel, won all of the money in the gang, and the kids booted him out, took the Gang House over, and run it on a better plan — there are some railroad trains and freight yard escapades, dust storms and Jungle camps that I've seen on the California river bottoms, hobo politics, kangaroo courts, and tales of the Mexican Border, the Oil Boom Towns, the thousands of people that deserted their little farms to get big wages in the Oil Fields, the "Boom Chasers" that were born right after Tobacco Road, and just before the Grapes of Wrath — in fact, by george, just come to think about it, I believe that's a good name for my book, "Boom Chasers." (It's kind of a book of short stories that all make one big story.)

I've finally rung the bell on this typewriter, so will let you know how I came out when I get in . . . (wait, that wasn't the typewriter bell, that was a alarm clock a going off. I suppose it will come back after while. By george it's morning, folks are all getting up and wishing they could go to work. I feel like a snake in the dark, I mean a thief in the grass, I've set here all night just a loafin' round with this internal machine.)

ARVIN, Calif. — Will Geer, Chuck Gordon, Harold Pfithjer, Herta Geer, and me put on some high powered, left handed, entertainment here 2 nights. I was told by numbers of people that the Picket Line was twice as long and twice as thick, and twice as strong — after Geer's Entertainers hit town.

The skit we put on was about a farmer with 2 sacks of spuds who had no pants and a Tailor with 2 pairs of pants, but nothin to eat — . They work to produce pants and potatoes, but are hungry and are cold. They finally spy each other, and decide to trade pants for spuds. An honest swap. But — as they proceed to cross a river to trade with each other, the middleman steps up in the middle of the bridge — stops them both — won't let them pass.

He demands "all" of the Farmer's Spuds, and even the pants the tailor has got on. He gives the farmer one pair of pants for 2 sacks of spuds, the tailor one sack of spuds for 2 pairs of pants. Thus, the middleman ends up with half the pants, half the spuds — and does no useful work whatever.

Herta Geer tells the whole story very interestingly, while Chuck Gordon plays the pantsless farmer, and Harold Pfithjer the hungry tailor . . . Will Geer plays the greedy middleman, and sings a belching song about Profits.

In the end Herta asks, Now . . . what would YOU DO. . . . " Well, they're going to do it, too!

The greedy middleman is picked up by the seat of the pants and thrown into the river . . . and the audience howls with a mysterious delight.

More and more of this sort of fun has got to be furnished for striking workers. It peps them up, bolsters their spirit of unity and brings them laughing and singing down to the Cotton Patch

YA GOTTA PICK
A LOT OF
COTTON
TO SMOKE A 5¢
CEEGAR!

After an original drawing by Woody Guthrie

or Warehouse Gate, or Factory Door — and it also keeps down hard personal feelings among the workers, that causes good men to drift away from the movement, and breeds weakness.

You don't have to depend on Hollywood for your entertainment, either. In the Cotton Strike they're making their own songs and skits, and the girls and the women are decoratin stages — and you'd be surprised what good talent you'll see there. With the friendliness of large Democratic Groups and Clubs in the bigger towns — financial help — and group tours — good will trips — etc., the Migratory Farm Workers can succeed very wonderfully at Unionism. This year, I think, more than ever, they have a chance — to get fair and honest treatment from the tightwad fist of the Associated Farmers.

"Tobacco Road" is closing in N.Y. after breaking all endurance records for hungry farmers and lady preachers. Will Geer is a farmer at heart. Studied plant husbandry in college. He's got him a big garden out here in the country. Pretty good at it, too. He's the only man I know of that knows these vegetables by their maiden names. He sticks his head out of the window and hollers about two dollars worth of Latin, and you know, them vegetables just come a running and jump in the stew pot. So if Will can't make a farm pay on Tobacco Road, the average dirt farmer aint got a chance. They wouldn't of had no Grapes of Wrath if it hadn't of been for Tobacco Road. The cast is got some new faces in it since I seen it last. But they aint all new to the Road. Howard Barnhart, Captain Tim, and fresh from the Boston Company last fall, is on Broadway now. Ashley Cooper is back again as old man Peabody. Lov is played by Marlon Willis, from Virginia, he's played it twice on the road, once on a show boat that sunk, and now back on 49th Street again. Bob Ross is still bouncing that dam tennis ball up against the side of the house, running his old ma, Miss La Berthone, ragged. Viny Phillips is still showing how the good sister Bessie tried to break Jetter of stealin' and Dude from cussin', and a driving that $800 car. All good champions deserve a big hand. So let's scatter a bale of hay and have a celebration and give good old Tobacco Road a big hand. The dirt farmers and the workers are the champions of the world, and some day we'll bring new life to the rotten, deserted farm houses along the back roads and Tobacco Roads of this country.

Seen the pitcher last night, Grapes of Wrath, best cussed pitcher I ever seen.

The Grapes of Wrath, you know is about us a pullin' out of Oklahoma and Arkansas, and down south, and a driftin' around over state of California, busted, disgusted, down and out, and a lookin' for work.

Shows you how come us to be that a way. Shows the dam bankers men that broke us and the dust that choked us, and comes right out in plain old English and says what to do about it.

It says you got to get together and have some meetins, and stick together, and raise old billy hell till you get youre job, and get your farm back, and your house and your chickens and your groceries and your clothes, and your money back.

Go to see Grapes of Wrath, pardner, go to see it and don't miss.

You was the star in that picture. Go and see your own self and hear your own words and your own song.

You know what a artist is dont you? A artist is a person that got out of a job so blame long they learnt to do something else.

Jesse James is a good picture —

'Course I have to wait till it gits down to the dime shows, but its a good picture anyhow —

(After all, I reckon a dime is worth 40c to me . . . they must be awful scarce. I see where the Finance outfits are charging four bits for a dime.)

The Railroad Racketeers hired Hoodlums & Thugs to beat and cheat the farmers out of their farms — and make em sell em for $1 an acre.

Frank & Jesse robbed the train to get even. They robbed it so often that the engineer was disappointed on days they coodent get there.

The Railroad President offered $25.00 for one of Jesse's own men to shoot him in the back. Robert Ford, a dirty coward, done the job . . .

Jesse's Tombstone read: Here Lies Jesse James, shot down by a dirty coward whose name is not worthy to appear here. . . . No wonder folks likes to hear songs about the Outlaws — they're wrong allright, but not ½ as dirty and sneakin' as some of our so-called "higher-ups" . . .

WOODY SEZ: ANY SONG THAT POINTS OUT SOMETHING WRONG
(Letter to Editors)

Dear Everybody:

Better late than never. I want to put my nickel in about Boogie Woogie.

We been house-hunting with them three kids and the landlords told us everything but welcome. Well, some day these kids will be landlords, but I doubt if them landlords was ever kids. I think they was just born old and stayed that a way.

But about Boogie Woogie. I just come from New York and you know everything there is six feet deep in Boogie Woogie and plumb soaked with music. You hear everything from African drums, to left-handed pipe organs.

I caint remember that word that Harrison George called Boogie so I will just fall back on Oakie dialectics. The Blues is rock bottom American music and was first made by Negroes and always was one of their strongest ways of protesting against slave conditions, plantation slavery or low-wage slavery, and there are bibles and bibles full of these songs filed away in the American Folk Music Division of the Library of Congress where no Congressmen will ever look or listen.

Under the present rich-man system, the working man hears his own voice so seldom that many very good labor strategists dont even recognize it as complete as he ought to.

The best way to get to knowing any bunch of people is go and listen to their music. John Steinbeck says, "You can burn books, etc., but you cannot stop their singing . . . there are still the spirituals of the slaves that say in effect, it is hopeless here, maybe in heaven it will be nicer . . . "

Most Forceful Blow

The Negro people were not allowed to talk out openly their hopes, their beliefs and their misery; so they fell back, I mean they stepped forward, and with their blues and spiritual songs, made stories and rhymes using all sorts of bugs, animals, trees, rivers, everything with which they were all familiar, and in this way struck a more forceful blow at their oppressor than pamphlets, books, or sermons.

Any song that points out something that is wrong, needs fixing, and shows you how to fix it — is the undying song of the working people. If it is made a little jazzy or sexy that aint wrong — what book could you read to a crowd that would make them dance?

I've seen great big two-fisted oil field drillers brought to tears just by listening to Blues and Boogie Woogie, because it made him think of some hard luck or calamity that struck his people; maybe he couldn't trace his troubles back to Wall Street, but he knew one thing: That song, them words, that tune told his story, said what he had to say, and whoever sings that song, or even plays the tune — he's with them, they're on the same side, no matter what happens.

The Blues Creep In

John L. Lewis said something to this effect, "The winning army is the singing army . . . ", and when working people sing their songs, their songs of protest and survival, hard-hitting songs of hard work and hard times, and then their fighting union songs, you're going to find the

Blues creeping into most of them, and from the Blues, Boogie.

So I say, Harrison, that as a judge of working class music you are a good editor of a worker's paper, let each spark plug fire its own cylinder. True as the average — Woody Guthrie, L.A., Calif.

Poor day today. Din't write but 3 Union Songs. Oh, well, that'll keep the deputy song writers busy another 6 months. Pete's even taking a whack at song making. He plowed out a couple yesterday. You know, you are as good a song writer as there is, but you might not believe it. If you dont believe it, that's why you're not. All you got to do is to set down and write up what's wrong and how to fix it. That's all there is to it. Lord knows there is plenty of matter to work on. All we need is more song writers. You, for instance. Naw, come on, it dont even have to rhime. Dont even have to be spelt right. All you got to do is just cut loose and let her roll out on paper, and when you get down something that's haywire and how to fix it, you got a song. Best part is, you dont even have to be able to write. You dont even have to be able to hum, whistle, or sing. You just got to speak it. That's all. Just whale away and yell it right out. Loud as you can. So somebody else can hear what's haywire and how to fix it. Then, you got a song. Every word is a music note of some kind, so ever thing you yell is a song. Geetars and banjos aint what makes the world go 'round. It's talkin' songs, and yellin' songs — and the best song, you dont even have to yell it. You just double up your fists, roll up your sleeves, and thump it out — on any convenient silk hat.

A brother asked me last night, Say, Woody, do you really write this stuff or is there somebody else sort of re-hashing it for you? And I says, well, by george, they is a big mystery there, allright. Inasmuch as some of my best cuss words are left out when the paper hits the streets.

He said, I dont want to hurt your feelings, but have you got a gag man? Derned if I know — but I know one thing for sure, I been gagged all of my life.

I got a big memorandum journal that I carry around with me. It has a big round pencil attached to it by a string. It's called a "date book." It helps me not to forget to remember, viz., i.e., et

all, that I have to be some place at a certain time
on a certain evening. Other folks has managers,
publicity men, agents, and secretaries to do all
this, but I'm still in the Ice Age as far as Big Technique goes. I just happen to look into that book (I
got another Memo Book that tells me just when to
look into the Date Book) and it says that I'm due
to sing, dance, recite, speak and otherwise
plague a crowd of people that's coming to the
Midtowners' Fall Frolic at the Hotel Monterey,
94th St., & Bdwy., tomorrow (Sat.) night. They
say lots of literary celebs will be there. I'll be there
to look everybody over — unless I get lost in
traffic.

Organ grinder down on the street below my
window, grinding out the "Sidewalks of New
York."

Mighty purty song.

Lots of folks here, just like the West Coast, a
grinding and a grinding away, a trying to grind
out a honest living.

This grinding is a mighty big organ, and out of
all of our grinding is goin' to come a song.

Out of all of our hard work and low pay, and
tired backs, and empty pocketbooks, is goin' to
come a tune.

And that song and that tune aint got no end, and it aint got no notes wrote down and they aint no piece of paper big enough to put it down on.

Every day you are down and out, and lonesome, and hungry, and tired of workin' for a hoboes handout, theys a new verse added to the song.

Every time you kick a family out of a house, cause they ain't got the rent, and owe lots of debts, why, theys another verse added to this song.

When a soldier shoots a soldier, thats a note to this song. When a cannon blows up 20 men, thats part of the rhythm, and when soldiers march off over the hill and dont march back, that's the drumbeat of this song.

This aint a song you can write down and sell.

This song is everywhere at the same time.

Have you ever heard it?

I have.

9 Folks
is a lookin
for freedom

You know what REACTION is dont you?

Well, when you make up a big batch of home-brew, and then it brews around too long, and goes sour on you . . . thats reaction.

I reckon re-action wood come under the head of action, allright, but it is a graspin action.

Kinda like a gettin choked. That's action, but it aint a very comfertable action.

Choppin a budget ½ in two wood be re-action.

A giving the relief folks a chancet to go to work on their own hook to earn their own keeps wood be action.

To hobble em and turn em out like a bunch of crippled horses wood be re-action.

A fightin the poore folks is re-action. And a fightin for the poore folks is action.

When youre car runs front ways, thats action. But when it pops, stutters, heaves, moans, groans, and backfires, and runs about 7000 revolutions backwards, why thats re-action.

(Stop me any time, editer.)

A re-action man is a man that acts just exactly bassakwards.

Over in Hollerwood, its Lights, Camera, and Action. Up in the Senate, its often — dark, secret, and re-action.

Looks like I caint keep out of the papers. When I was born they had to make out the papers. When you roll a smoke you got to have the papers. When you come acrost a state line they want your papers. When you by a jallopy you got to get the papers. When you get married, its papers an when you get a devorce its papers and when you marry agin its more papers an when you die its papers papers papers.

When you get a job you got papers. When you get on relief its papers — your papers, your paw's papers, youre ma's papers, your grandparents papers an their neighbor's papers.

When Hitler an Musclini gets together they draw up papers. Then Mr. Lamechamber comes along and they make out some more papers. Then Mr. Stalin comes down an they tear up all the old papers. Mr. Roosevelt comes along an they all hook up an make out some more peace pack papers — an when all of em get home they tear up all of the papers an Mr. Hearst puts it down to suit him in his own paper and Mr. Rockyfeller loses some oil papers an Mr. Dupont some compny papers an the millionaires get in a squabble about the mineral papers an yell for the workin folks to come join the war an its in all the papers.

An even before you can go over an get shot properly you got to have volanteer papers an enlistment papers an training papers an passport papers an — gosh my heads a whirlin — but it'll be in the papers.

IT IS WHISPERED A ROUND THAT I AM EXPECTING A BABY . . .

Aint seen no doctor yet, cause we aint got what the dr. likes to see . . . the money.

A dr. is a person that has got to make a living . . . but he'll take in one night what it takes me six months to get.

I aint never been werth much sense I been here, I wonder how come it cost so much to get here?

What can a dr. do in ½ a night that's worth six months of scratchin, and diggin, and skimpin, and skippin, and savin, and playing on the radeo waves?

I guess you got some special kind of work you do, just like I have . . . and I guess you have, or someday will, have two or three children . . . just like I have.

Funny how one feller can hit a few licks of some sort of 'inspired work' like a doctor, or a lawyer, and take all of the inspiration out of you for a year.

I heard of a woman having 19 babies and not a docter. I bet she was a liberal. The only thing these drs. are liberal with is duns and bills.

It may be worth $4 or $5 or maybe $10 (carpenters wages) — to deliver a baby — but, gosh, that aint the hard part of raisin children.

The drs. want anywhers from $50 to $200 for a new model, streamline job — and I just natural think you ott to make the $200 check out to the mother in the deal, and give the doc $10 (cement finisher wages) — and kiss him goodnight, and wish him good luck in his "inspired work for humanity."

NEW YORK — A lady called me up over the fone wires today and says, hello, is this you?

And I says, I guess so, I'll feel and see.

And she says, say, I'm a nurse.

And I said, well, how's dizziness?

She said, I called you up to see where I could get a hold of you.

I says, you must be a awful young nurse.

She said, no, you see a bunch of doctors and nurses are a having a party to celebrate being in debt, and we want you to be our guest of honor.

I says, well, as for debt, you got the right man, but what is a guest of honor?

And she says, oh, a guest of honor just comes

and visits us and makes us a little talk and sings us a little song and help us to have a good time.

I says, lady, thats a mighty slick way to ask me to work free, but if your politics is right, and theys any eats left, I'll be there.

Dear Everybody:

Say when I left New York to go to Oklahoma, I got a letter from a Dentist there in the city with a statement that I owed him Five Dollars for a Tooth he Pulled. Now, I remember all about this tooth, although I was somewhat doped on dope at the time, and I remember just how he yanked it out, and how he got his knees on my belly and how he left me feeling like half of my head was gone, and I admit I was groggy, but I wasn't unconscious, this is important, as I recall clearly that he took the tooth between some pinchers or pullers, and he laid it up on a shelf there in his office, and now he says I owe him for the tooth, and I swear I left it laying right there on that shelf.

No, I was just a teething, I really do owe him $5 for the $1 worth of work he done for me, I hadn't ought to be a hog about this. And I always get his letters when I ain't got the money, and when I get a little money, he don't say a word about it, so maybe someday I'll get five bucks in my clothes, and hear from him that same day.

Maybe

Aint shaved since I left New York. Giving my face and stomach a rest. If I had a dog or horse that shaved I'd say he was batty, but us men has got to do it to make a living — wonder who the hell started that? Whoever he was, I'm really cheating on him these days.

Well the WPA got cut 55 per cent they tell me. That was a devil of a swath. I remember the first airplane that ever flew over our old home town, Okemah, Okfuskee County, Oklahoma, well — it scared all of the teams of horses, and they humped up and backed up, and kicked a loose from the harness, and they had about 17 runaway teams there, a thundering up alleys, and down streets, and out across the horse trading lots, and clipped the corners off of half of the stores in town, and strung boards off of the old frame drug stores and saloons, and run through stacks of chicken coops out in front of the stores, and got the coops and the chickens all hung up in the wagon wheels, and between the feathers, winchester rifle smoke, and dust, you couldnt see a cussed thing around that town for 10 days.

You know the preachers raise cane about a lot of things, but they seldom (about like me) approach the problem of the day, its handling, or its solution, its cause, its starting place, its present condition, or probable outcome.

I am sure that, should The Master appear again on airth, that He would take a look at the churches, a look at the sinners and associate himself at once with the sinners . . . as He did before. Religion is to forget yourself and work for the good of others. Outside of that there is no religion . . . no progress . . . no hope — for you, your neighbor, your coming grandchildren.

Find out who is causing the Trouble here in this old World — remove the Power from their hands — place it in the hands of those who aint Greedy — and you can rooll over and go to sleep.

I AINT GOT NOTHIN A GINST TH CHURCHES, BUT YOU CAINT PILE UP A PILE OF ROCKS AN CALL IT RELIEGION. IF A PILE OF CEMENT AN SAND HAD ANYTHING TO DO WITH RELIGION, EVER MOUNTEN IN TH COUNTRY WOOD BE STILL BETTER.

Personal, I ruther carry on my services out here on some mt. then to depend on a church to help me. I dont know what they got hemmed up in there, but whatever it is — I dont kneed it.

Lots of folks thinks th gospel is a thing a bout

as big as a dime — that youre on it one day, an off of it th next — er a circle a bout th size of a big marble rigring — an one day youre in it, an th next day youre out of it — well I got me sort of a one man religion — but it takes in everybody — an my religion is so big, no matter who you are, youre in it, an no matter what you do you caint git out of it.

I dont think th sky specially cares what th devil you do down here. Its purty liberal. Takes in a lots of countery, an over looks a lot of things — an makes everybodys money look like a silly pile of purty sea shells.

If theys anything that clouds th sky up — its youre own dern greed — an cause youre a frade — an cause you think two much a bout youreself . . . religion dont cause it . . . religion caint cure it . . . its youre own dern thinkin . . . either way you look at it.

WELL, you don't hear nothin' new after you hear your 1st preaching'.

Preachers is all right, fine and dandy, I use to want to be one, but you can learn more off of the kids. Even the preachers send you to the kids.

I still say — go to the kids, see the kids, study the kids, and be like the kids.

Some people whip the kids, but you stil caint beat em.

A child is a humen being before it gets all bawled up.

Freedom of religion is a good thing to talk about. I've talked to lots of preachers who tell me they haven't got any freedom of speech, and that if they would get up and preach the Truth and nothing but the Truth, padlocks would be hanging on their church doors in the morning . . . A Los Angeles bus driver that once was a preacher told me that he preached what he believed, about money, war, rich folks, poor folks, working folks, and leeches, and that he got booted out of his church. He said it was all under 'political control' — I used to leave him a copy of the People's World every day — on the bus — and he said, "That's what it ought to be, by gosh, the People's World!"

Workers of the world, it's either Unite or Untie, they both spell the same, but they's a whale of a difference.

While I wuz on the bum in Calif., I slept in everything but a bed.

I et ever thing except a square meal.

An found ever thing except a home.

I rode on everything that had wheels, from a one cylinder kiddy car to a mountain massey railroad locomotive.

I made ever thing except money an lost ever thing but my debts.

I aint a communist necessarily, but I have been in the Red all my life.

Lots of rich folks running away from honest work, lots running after it, some running for sheriff, some running from him.

Well, from what I've been abel to gether in my young life, money is power. Hole armies of people will do anything you tell em to, if you can show th 'long green'. You can buy you a yatch, an fill it plumb full of Standard gas & oil, an' Ralph's groceriews, an Frankfort's liquors, an' — well, jest any dern fool thing you want, if you can show 'em the 'long green.'

It don't make no diffrence where the heck you got it, jest so you got it. It dont make no diffrence who you robbed, but they have got some laws regulatin' how you rob 'em. They is 2 forms of robbin'. One is legal. The other is un-legal. But the main idee in this day an' time is to 'get all you can, and can all you get.'

Money is power. Because the Money Boys wants Money to be Power. An' as Long as the Money Boys are in Power, Money's will be Power — but the only trouble is — they wont be no money.

Because the Money Boys will keep on arguin', and a chewin' the rag amongst their selves, about who owns what, an' who rules who, an' who dictates to which, an' who controls what, ect., ect., ect.

An — they'll tear down their own system of Money Role if we'll jest give 'em time.

As long as a nation is run by, of, and for the Werkin' People, you got Progress.

As long as a natian is run by Money Rule, you got rotten politicians, rotten banks, rotten crops, rotten clothing, rotten gangsters, and rotten ever thing.

I dident know I was so smart. Woody.

A dollar bill is green, and when you're green you don't know. Other sides gray, and that's sometimes how it is when you do know.

OKLAHOMA CITY. — Burnt out the distributor on our purty car. Mechanic said it should of been greased or oiled or bribed or something. Well aint the National Distributor giving the same trouble?

They's lots of good ideas in a pint of Port Wine, but not so many in a quart.

Just seen Hank Fonda in "The Return of Frank James." Round about way its better than Jesse James. My favorite actor is a mixture between Henry Fonda, Errol Flynn, Spence Tracy, Will Rogers and Mickey Rooney. You know, sort of all wrapped up in one. After all Willkie can out act any of them but Hank Fonda can out spit Willkie. Errol Flynn can out climb him, Spence Tracy can out fight him, and Mickey Rooney can cut more monkey shines, and too boot, I'd about as soon have Jesse James for President.

Folks that's been in Foreign Countries can't help it. They went to a lot of work and trouble a gettin' here — most of us is here by accident, anyway . . . but the fellers that jump on you and make trouble for you just because of the place you was born . . . well, all I got to say is, that 2,000 years ago we had 'em, and we got plenty of 'em right now, and 2,000 years from now they'll be out arresting you and a having your trial, a trying to prove you was born up on the moon.

If you don't believe it, just clip this column, and in the year 3940 A.D., remember I warned you.

Shucks, plague take it, no how — grabbed up the newspaper today and turned into it, and thought to my soul I'd run onto something. It looked at first glance like a map of the U.S., which it was. It had all 48 states. With big black dots on it, all over it, and some of the dots was half black and half white — with big mean looking arrows winding out across the country like a copper head snake chasing a young bull frog — and just at first glance. I thought it was the "probable" line of this "probable" invasion, and the "probable" towns they would "probable" try to take, and the "probable" place you could "probable" hem 'em all up, and "probable" catch 'em, and thrash the hound out of 'em, and how you "probable" whim wham their ships and submarines faster'n they could "probable" ship 'em over — from Portland, Maine, to Portland, Oregon, from Lost Angeles, to Miami, and "probable" other places.

Then I read down there below it, and it said it wasn't nothing but a weather map with the "probable" way the wind would blow.

Two Kinds of Newspapers in the world. A feller told me the other day that he liked to read his papers before he had breakfast. That's one kind.

Another kind is for you to read when you ain't got no breakfast, a paper that tells you who's got your breakfast.

Books is all right. Far as books go, but as far as they go, they still don't go far enough. A book is just like a womans dress, short enough to be interesting, and long enough to cover the subject.

Cornbread is my text for today. Since I been in New York I've rarely been able to run acrost any cornbread like it was back home. Up here they put it 2–3 flour and 1–3 sugar and I've even found it fell so low as to have raisins in it. This is called cake in the west.

What this world needs is a little roughage. Thats the key secret of a raising good husky radical livestock, and the same goes for people.

Flour cornbread with sugar, is too slick to stick to your ribs, and too smooth to tickle your stomach, and has a tendency to let things go by too easy — and roughage is the thing thats needed — it is the thing that will bring you more groceries. After that, you can decorate as you please.

This artickle was produced under the influence of the second pone 9 × 12 × 18, which was cooked in ¼ inch of hog lard by a lady, ex-cowgirl, from the wild and wooly Texas plains, where the landscape itself looks like one big pan of cornbread.

As to this business of phony psychology, I've talked with thousands of people about every kind of a booger man imaginable. Spirits, Witches, The Evil Eye, Trance Mediums, Wonder Workers, Miracle Men, Master Minds, Telepathists, Projectionists, Star Gazers, Hell Raisers, Cloud Riders, Night Gliders, Astrologists, Cosmicologists, Magnetic Healers, Faith Healers, Mind Readers, Fortune Tellers, Luck Bringers, Truth Tellers. Haints, Saints, Pintos, Paints — yet, I was deeply and seriously interested in these things for several years — all kinds of Mysticism. Mind Science, Christian Science, Unity Diviners of all sorts and sizes. I think that some of you good readers, writers and left-handed thinkers had ought to realize that this is the field that had ought to be exposed for what it is worth; that superstition and witchery is one of the greatest forces today that cripples the people's movement. It teaches you to put your trust and all of your hope in something somewhere, nothing. It breeds the wildest kind of fear in the imagination.

Feller asked me if I was a Folk Lorist, and I said — Nope, I'm a Poor Folkist.

A man's ambition is little of him, that'll always run to the boss and tell, a woman's love is often little and it's a libel that they tattle, I started to say "tittle" to rime with "little" — but switched to "tattle" to rime with "prattle," 'cause tit for tit and tat for tat, a scabbers heart beats awful flat.
Poet and rarin to show it.

Grapes of Wrath is a playin to Oklahoma theatres. I hear they are half empty. Too bad. Well the old world don't like to smell its own B.O., and besides, us "Oakies" aint got the two bits to go on, and the "bloakies" that robbed us dam sure don't want a vision of it a lookin' em right square in the face. Both sides are a standing there, the hungry ones and the bloated ones, and the preacher says, "Now boys, be calm, for in reality, the other aint there . . . "

A JAPANESE FAMILY LIVES ON THE FRONT OF THIS LOT . . . their name is Hanio, Hanyo, or Hanjo — or something — I aint never been abel to spell it yet.

Anyhow, the father and mother came over to the United States from acrost the ocean. And the father calls all of his daughters and sons around him and tells them they ott to be proud to live in a country where you can be free to work, and earn your livin, and go anywheres you want to, and say anything you want to.

He tells them about life over acrost the ocean — hard work, long hours, low wages, bum houses, starvation, and everthing, and I dont think this family know or take pride in anything that is a takin place over there now.

He says, they's more freedom over here in a day then they is over there in a year. And he was born and raised so poore, so hungery, and so held down — that it is good to hear him brag on the U.S.A.

Folks is a lookin for FREEDOM. Here and hereafter, the best thing they ask for is FREEDOM. A job of WORK, a fair CHANCE, an HONEST SHARE of the stuff they perduce . . . HONEST PAY for the WORK they do . . . they got that much a comin to em, and they are dadgum shure a goin to GET IT. They'll cross oceans, fight wars, migerate like birds, go through hell's high waters, or anything else 1000 times — to get FREEDOM.

That's how come the U.S.A. to get started — and that's what has kept her a goin . . . FREEDOM.

The Fall of the year is nearly here and Summer's had it's day, and 'twont be long till Winter Time will come to visit and stay, like relatives that come along, or men of might and main, that somehow get in office, and then wont get out again; but time rolls on and while she rolls, the calender goes around and everywhere you look about, below and under ground, above on high, and in the sky, and all around the town, there rolls along a Union strong. The fall will fall and winter wilt, and spring will come again, and summer smother some of us, and roll on 'round again, and Roosevelt and Willkie and all the Rich

Guys Crowd will age and grow, but well, you know, they're on their last go 'round!

I guess you've heard about as many wild and windy Cyclone Tales as I have. An' I guess you've seen as many Cyclones in operation as I have. But the thousands of letters on thet very subjict thet come into me at KFVD, has prooved to me that ever body likes to stop an' hear a good tall, handsome, wild, an' windy Cyclone Tale oncet in a while.

The One I want to scribble here this mornin' is sposed to be a fact, as facts seem to be purty stretchy outfits. An' this is one of the stretchiest I cood git a holt of.

Jim Lukas was a boilin' an' a scrapin' a hog one mornin' down in the cow lot when a Cyclone struck, Jim laid his big long butcher knife up on a barrel, an' made a run for the storm cellar.

You know, that cyclone hit, an' grabbed that knife up in its Twister, an' boiled an' scraped four more your shoats, sliced 'em up into bacon, pork chops, back-bone, hogs-head, an' chitlin's, salted it all down an' carried the knife off.

It struck again over on the next 40, an' plugged 4 acres of watermellons for Bill Keefer; dug an' peeled 14 rows of Irish 'taters for Mrs. Keefer; cut the Oklahoma state budget half in two; headed 20 acres of kafir corn for Lem Hughes, and cut old man Jones' water off.

Wait a minit, I ain't through. It cut the Indian's allowance down 30 per cent, made a big split in the Republican Party, sliced 3 barrells of "pork" for the Lobbyists; cut down half on WPA checks; cut relief plumb out of that county . . . shaved 3 deputy sheriffs . . . an' tore down 4 of the best likker stills on the Canadian River bottom.

That was some blow!

GEORGE is my brother. And he's in love. He's just a comin' 21.

The Girls name is Harriet . . . the reason they call her Harriet is because that's her name. It wood be a waste of time to call her something else when Harriet is her name.

I ott to know her name well . . . George has wrote it on the wall more times than the Examiner cood of.

Give him a good pencil, and a good even break and he cood write her name more times than England cood write Peace Packs.

George — he is just a ripening into what you wood call "That Certain Age" — you know, when you walk around with a far away look in your eyes, and run over boxes, and stumble over furniture, and walk into telaphone poles, and act as absent minded as a Senator a Slicing a Budget.

When youre heart beats about four times assss fast asss it ott to, and the Dr. caint do a thing a bout it. When youre blood runs thru your veins like a speedway and the Police caint fix it. When youre eyes get set in youre head like a crying calf, and youre a floatin along in the clouds — plum out of this world.

Well, that's sort of how old George is . . . sence he fell in love.

He wants a good suit of clothes, a sport coat, new shoes, haircuts, face lotion, perfume, clean socks . . . and a Car . . . and plenty of plain and fancy Highways, Side Roads, Beaches, and Parks.

Young folks in Love has got this much a comin' to 'em.

I wood favor a bill in Congress as the "Young Billers & Cooers Bill" No. 18,999,000 — which wood hire 1,000,000 Investigators & Special Detectives to go out and hunt up everybody in Love and get their name and address, and send 'em a good Used Car — tailored to fit —

And in the back seat they ott to receive the Complete Layout of Good Flashy clothes — to — well just receive em, that's all.

And then we ott to hire 1,000,000 more Investigators and Policemen to arrest and deport from the United States the first Finance Credit Man that sought, by usury, and outrageous interest rates — to enslave, degrade, depress, deprive, and otherwise "rob" our young folks that's a fallin in Love, and a gettin married.

The KKK gangs are a coming out on a bronc, schute No. 3, rider No. 7, but I'll lay 2 to one he gets throwed. Anybody that's yellow enough or 2 faced enough to have to put a sack over his head to do his dirty work, well, he just caint win, 'cause he caint see good enough . . . the world just don't operate that a way. . . . Anybody that gets so far off track as to go around with a sack over his head is just to lose out, well, just because he don't believe in what he's a doing, and it's hard enough to win, as we all know, even with our bare face a hanging out, even when you're right.

Stayed a few nights with a artist and painter by trade, and he's got a mighty good picture of a lynching a hanging on my right wall. I mean my right hand, and it shows you one man, a Negro

man, already hung for excitement and entertainment, and another'n being drug in and beat up
with clubs and chains and fists and guns — and
so naturally I caint think up no jokes for today.
This painting is so real I feel like I was at a lynching, and it somehow or other just takes all of the
fun and good humor and good sport out of you to
set here and realize that people could go so haywire as to hang a human body up by a gallus pole
and shoot it full of Winchester rifle holes just for
pastime. It reminds me of the postcard picture
they sold in my home town for several years, a
showing you a negro mother, and her two young
sons, a hanging by the neck from a river bridge,
and the wild wind a whistling down the river
bottom, and the ropes stretched tight by the
weight of their bodies and — the rope stretched
tight like a big fiddle string. Aint no telling how
many will march by the songs that have whistled
through the ribs of the poor lynch victims.

Life has got a habit of not standing hitched.
You got to ride it like you find it. You got to
change with it. If a day goes by that dont change
some of your old notions for new ones, that is
just about like trying to milk a dead cow.

If you're too bull headed to change your old

notions for the ones that come up every morning,
you belong over in the herd with the ones that are
herded around like cattle.

If I ever die don't bury me
On Wall Street under a cement tree
Where folks can look at a marble slab
And all of this trash and obstructory,
But if I die and when I do,
Just cart me out where the sky is blue,
And have some carrier carve this piece:
Woody knows just where he is.

Notes

Woody Guthrie wrote in his time and for his people. His columns turned on his personal experiences and on events occurring daily in the world. His writings were intelligible to his readers in spite of deliberate misspellings, but some references may be obscure to the younger reader. These notes are an attempt to clarify when clarification seems to be needed.

Aunt Molly Jackson was the wife of a leader of a United Mine Workers Local in Harlan County, Kentucky.

Bill. Bill Guthrie was Woody's third child and first son, born in 1940.

Bob Wood, a friend of Woody's, was an organizer for the Oil Workers Union in Oklahoma.

Boogie-Woogie, a vital style of blues played on the piano (with a running bass).

"Boom Chasers" was the working title of Woody's autobiography. It was published in 1943, under the title *Bound for Glory*.

Cisco Houston, like Woody, a performer and composer, was Woody's closest buddy. During the Second World War he served with Woody in the Merchant Marine.

Dust Bowl Ballads: While in New York City in 1940, Woody recorded an album titled *Dust Bowl Ballads* for RCA Victor Record Company. This, his first "commercial" album, quickly became a collector's item: sales were insignificant. Not until 1964 did RCA Victor re-release the album as part of its "Vintage" series. A limited number of records were pressed, and again it became a collector's item.

Ed Robbin was a young journalist in Los Angeles who doubled as a news commentator for *People's World*, broadcasting daily on the independent radio station KVFD. Woody, in that spring of 1939, also had a radio program on the station, singing and playing the guitar. The program, then classified as "western music and cowboy songs," was aired just before Robbin's. Woody and Ed met almost every day, and they became friendly. It was Woody who asked Robbin if his newspaper would accept a column. Some weeks passed before the editors of *People's World* accepted Woody Guthrie as a columnist.

The Grapes of Wrath, by John Steinbeck, portrayed Okies in the years of the dust bowls, people with whom Woody could and did feel a powerful identification. He had traveled with people like the Joad family. "Tom Joad" — one of the longest ballads

Woody ever wrote — is a six-minute retelling of this story. It was written after Woody saw the movie.

Ham & Egger: A California populist movement of the late 1930s that advocated pension plans for the elderly. The movement was confined to California.

Harness guards: A reference to the big, fat railroad police who tried to keep the down-and-out from riding the freight trains.

Harrison: Harrison George, an editor of *People's World*.

Lamechamber: Neville Chamberlain, then Prime Minister of England.

Leadbelly. Huddie Ledbetter, a former sharecropper and a prodigious blues singer, and "king of the twelve-string guitar," had served a prison term on a Texas chain gang. He was released through the efforts of John Lomax, the folklorist. Leadbelly, best known for the songs he wrote, was a great musical influence on Woody. Woody met him in New York City in 1940, and came to look to him for inspiration.

John L. Lewis was without doubt the most important labor leader of the 1930s and 1940s. As president of the United Mine Workers, he became the founding president of the Congress of Industrial Organizations (CIO) to "organize the unorganized," along industrial lines, instead of, as in the AFL, along craft lines.

Mother Bloor: Ella Reeve Bloor was the Grand Old Lady of the radical movement in the 1930s. She was involved in many labor struggles, and gained national prominence when she became active in the Communist party.

Musclini: Benito Mussolini, dictator in fascist Italy.

Olson: Culbert Olson was governor of California from 1938 to 1942.

"our third time round": A reference to Franklin D. Roosevelt's race for a third term as President.

Pete: Pete Seeger, the well-known folk singer, whom Woody met for the first time in 1940.

Spanish refugees: Loyalists to the Spanish Republic who fled from Spain after Franco defeated the Republican Army in 1939.

Union Square, a park on east 14th Street in New York City, was the major center for soap box oratory. Speakers stood on boxes — with the American flag displayed — and gathered small and large groups of listeners, depending on the interest in the topic and the ability of the orator. Everything and anything could be heard in Union Square, with as many as twenty-five orators speaking at once.

Wall Street, the center of world finance in the 1930s (as it still is today), represented to Woody — and to many Americans of the time — the maneuverings of the industrial and financial world at the expense of the working people.

Walter Winchell: An influential gossip columnist and radio commentator with a vast following in the 1930s and 1940s — and a Red-baiter.

Will Geer, today a well-known character actor for his role in *The Waltons* television series, was married at this time to Herta Geer. Chuck Gordon and Harold Pfithjer were young actors who worked with him in Geer's Entertainers. Geer had played the lead on Broadway in *Tobacco Road,* a dramatization of the lives of poor farm people.

Willkie: Wendell Willkie, Republican candidate for president in the 1940 election.

W.P.A.: Works Progress Administration, set up in 1933 by the Roosevelt administration to create public jobs with federal funds.